SP

Fairs Fair   E&F   **$10.00**

0739445545

Austin, Denise

Sculpt Your Body with Balls and Bands

D0573654

SCULPT YOUR BODY

WITH

BALLS

AND

BANDS

DENISE AUSTIN

STAR OF *THE DAILY WORKOUT* AND *FIT & LITE*, *Lifetime*®
Television for Women®

SCULPT YOUR BODY

WITH

BALLS

AND

BANDS

SHED POUNDS AND GET FIRM

IN 12 MINUTES A DAY

RODALE®

Notice

This book is intended as a reference volume only, not as a medical manual. The information given here is designed to help you make informed decisions about your health, diet, fitness, and exercise program. It is not intended as a substitute for professional fitness and medical advice. If you suspect that you have a medical problem, we urge you to seek competent medical help. As with all exercise programs, you should seek your doctor's approval before you begin.

Mention of specific companies, organizations, or authorities in this book does not imply endorsement by the publisher, nor does mention of specific companies, organizations, or authorities imply that they endorse this book.

Internet addresses and telephone numbers given in this book were accurate at the time it went to press.

© 2004 by Denise Austin
Illustrations © 2004 by Rodale Inc.

All rights reserved. No part of this publication may be reproduced or transmitted in any form or by any means, electronic or mechanical, including photocopying, recording, or any other information storage and retrieval system, without the written permission of the publisher.

Printed in the United States of America

ISBN 0-7394-4554-5

Illustrations by Phil Guzy
Interior photographs by Hilmar, except for the photo on page v (courtesy of the author) and before and after photos (courtesy of the individuals profiled)

Book design by Tara Long

To Jeff, Kelly, and Katie, whom I love every second of every day. . . .

CONTENTS

part
(3) **Your 3-Week Plan**

ACKNOWLEDGMENTS

More than anything, I love being with my family. Just hanging out with my "honeybunny" Jeff and our precious daughters, Kelly and Katie, makes me so happy. I thank God every day for their health and happiness. I love being a mom.

I still wish my mom were alive; I just simply miss her. She was my role model in life, so dedicated to all five of us kids. She had such a joyful attitude, and, boy, was she fun! . . . Thanks, Mom.

And to my dad for teaching me to work hard and believe in myself. Thanks for giving me the love of sports. (My dad played professional baseball in 1946 to 1947.)

I am forever grateful to all my sisters and my brother, that we truly care about each other and cherish our times together.

I want to thank all those who have helped me at Rodale, especially Tami Booth and my wonderful editor, Mariska Van Aalst. Thanks also to all my friends at *Prevention* magazine for "giving" me my own column. And thanks to Jan Miller and Michael Broussard, my literary agents . . . love you guys.

A big thanks to Alisa Bauman for making this book happen; you're a joy to work with. Thanks to my good friend Steve Kostorowski for all your help.

Thank you, Leslie Bonci, R.D., for your expertise in planning these nutritious meals.

While I was writing this book, I received a great honor: I was inducted into the Video Hall of Fame. It was an exciting evening, and I was able to share it with all my family and close friends. Thank you to all my friends at Lions Gate, home to my videos and DVDs, and especially to Steve Beeks . . . thanks for your unbelievable support . . . and yours, too, Lee Eiland—you're the best.

There are so many people to thank, especially my girlfriends who are always there for me. Thanks from the bottom of my heart.

PART 1

BALLS, BANDS, AND YOU

YOUR BODY, YOUR TIME, YOUR EFFORT

Sculpt a slimmer, toner you in 12 minutes a day

Tick, tock, tick, tock—the clock is always moving ahead, zooming us through jam-packed days, pulling us through months before we can even notice where the weeks have gone. Every day, I hear from busy women and men who tell me that every day feels like a hectic race, starting the moment the alarm clock sounds and ending the moment they crawl back into bed in an exhausted heap. They tell me that they *want* to do what it takes to lose weight. They know they need to exercise and eat right, but they don't know where to find the time to accomplish their personal goals while balancing family, career, and other responsibilities.

Does all of this sound familiar? Can you relate? I sure can. As a mother, a wife, and a busy career woman, I know all too well how challenging it can feel to try to carve out a chunk of personal time. My secret to success—and one I'd like to share with you—is placing *quality* ahead of quantity.

I try to stick to this simple philosophy in every aspect of my life. Each day, I strive for at least one good moment in which I can connect with my daughters and husband in a *meaningful* way. In the kitchen, I cook up quick and easy meals by picking just a few fresh, healthful ingredients. During my workouts, I concentrate on using the most effective equipment and routines, maximizing my results in a minimum amount of time. I know that time is our most precious resource, so I want to make every minute work for me.

That's why I'm so happy to tell you that you can sculpt your body and lose weight in just 12 minutes a day, with the help of two pieces of equipment that are quickly becoming the hottest fitness trends in the country. Stability balls and resistance bands are revolutionizing the fitness industry. I began using resistance bands more than 10 years ago and the stability ball more than 4 years ago, and I've always been impressed with the results. More recently, I combined the two pieces of equipment into a comprehensive, effective program, and I was amazed at what they could do for me. After just 12 minutes with the ball and bands, I had worked out every muscle in my body. It revolutionized the way I exercise.

Now I'd like to share this amazingly efficient system with you. My stability ball and resistance band program will help you shrink your waistline, slim your hips and thighs, and flatten your tummy—all in just 12 moves a day. You'll combine your daily 12-minute routines with my sensible, simple, and scrumptious eating plan that includes quick and easy meal options. Most of these mouthwatering low-carb meals can be prepared in well under—you guessed it—12 minutes!

You'll be astonished at how little time you'll need to experience dramatic results. Even more important, after you complete the 3-week plan in part 3, you'll feel the ultimate sense of accomplishment that comes from seamlessly integrating fitness into your life in a *meaningful* way that doesn't interfere with your roles as parent, friend, and employee.

Let's take a closer look at the equipment you'll be using, the inexpensive tools that make it all possible.

THE SECRET BEHIND THE BALL AND BANDS

Chances are, you've seen the large, colorful, air-filled vinyl balls that are becoming more popular at sporting goods stores and in gyms. Also called the Swiss ball, fitness ball, balance ball, and other names, this simple, yet effective, fitness tool got its start during the 1960s, in the physical therapy industry. The stability ball was originally used to help children with cerebral palsy and adult stroke victims to regain muscle control. Over the years, however, many physical therapists noticed that using the stability ball was also doing something else—it was helping these patients strengthen and tone their bodies, particularly the core muscles in the abdomen, back, waistline, thighs, and buttocks. Yet, it produced zero pounding or jarring to the joints, serving as a safe, fun, and *very effective* rehabilitation tool.

Over the years, the stability ball has rolled out of the doctor's office and into fitness centers across the country—and for good reason. Stability balls have limitless potential to create efficient, effective, and fun workouts. You'll be able to tone your trouble spots while you improve your balance and coordination, all the while zeroing in on your core—your abs, back, waist, hips, and butt—and working multiple muscle groups at once. In particular, the stability ball will help you to strengthen and tone those small, intricate muscles in your lower abdomen and pelvic girdle. That's important for women as it helps flatten the lower tummy, prevent incontinence, and even improve sexual satisfaction (ooh, la, la!).

When you exercise on the ball, you're using muscles throughout your body just to remain balanced. So, for example, if you lie on the ball as if it were a weight bench and do a set of chest presses, you not only work the muscles you are targeting in your chest but also tone your abdomen, waist, and back muscles as they work to keep you balanced, and your thigh and buttocks muscles as they support your body weight. Now that's what I call total-body exercise! Because the ball helps you use so many muscles at once in every single exercise, you can completely tone your muscles in much less time than with other exercise tools.

When you combine the stability ball with resistance bands, you increase the effectiveness of your workouts even more. Resistance bands provide the perfect complement to the stability ball; using them, you'll be able to simultaneously improve your flexibility and your strength.

You can stretch these latex bands to do just about any traditional strength-training or toning move that you would normally do with dumbbells, barbells, or exercise machines. As with dumbbells, the bands provide resistance, making your muscles work to overcome it. Because the bands stretch in any conceivable direction, however, you can tone and stretch your muscles through a greater range of motion than you could with traditional forms of resistance, creating a well-rounded workout. The bands and the ball allow you to move your body through multiple planes—forward, backward, and sideways. You can rotate, twist, and move in arcs and circles. These multidimensional movements help to sculpt beautiful muscles from head to toe and inside and out.

The bands also improve your coordination, because you must use your muscles in new ways to stay balanced as you stretch and release the band. What I really love about the bands, though, is that they are easy on the joints. They are the perfect choice for people with arthritis and other joint discomfort because they provide gentle, yet consistent, resistance through a wide range of motion. In fact, a good friend of mine, David Silver, M.D., chief of rheumatology at Cedars-Sinai Medical Center in Los Angeles, says that many people who avoid exercise because of joint pain can often exercise with resistance bands pain-free.

I truly believe that the stability ball and resistance bands are the most important exercise accessories for busy women and men. They enable you to reclaim your health and your life by allowing you to embark on a fitness and weight-loss plan that is entirely doable—you *can* and will get fit quickly and easily with this plan. Best of all, you can do it all in the privacy of your own home and even use your new fitness tools in many other ways. For example, by sitting on my stability ball instead of using a desk chair in my home office, I'm continually challenging my core muscles, getting exercise benefits while I type, chat on the phone, or read my e-mail. (In fact, I'm sitting on mine right now as I write this book.) What could be a better use of time?

You'll learn more about the incredible benefits of the stability ball and bands in chapter 2. Time's a-wasting, so let's get on to the Power of 12—the whole-life strategy that will help you win the battle with the ticking clock.

THE POWER OF 12

Here's the most exciting news about the stability ball and bands: You can sculpt your *entire body* in just 12 minutes. No kidding! I've found that 12 minutes is the perfect amount of time for a toning workout. If you work out for less time, you won't see results. If you work out for more time, you may bite off more than you can chew, get discouraged, and be unable to maintain your fitness routine.

If you've struggled to fit in workouts of 30 minutes or longer, I designed this program with you in mind. Have you started and stopped exercising numerous times before? Perhaps you stuck with it for 2 or 3 weeks but then skipped a workout . . . and then another . . . and then yet another. Eventually, you may have stopped exercising altogether. Don't beat yourself up or feel guilty! When you have a full schedule, it can be tough to find 30 minutes in a day to exercise. The good news is that you don't need to exercise for that long to see amazing results—you need only 12 minutes.

Let's be honest: 12 minutes is over before you know it. I'll bet you can find 12 minutes in your day. If you're like most people, that means setting the alarm clock 12 minutes earlier and getting up for your toning session. Get your workout out of the way in the morning, and you'll feel good about yourself for the rest of the day. You'll find that when you move in the morning, you tend to make better food choices and are more active throughout the day. Many people have told me that starting the day on the right foot helps them stay on the right foot. For example, Paula Shupe, who lost 42 pounds with consistent exercise, says, "When I work out first thing in the morning, I'm not taking any time away from my family and friends, and therefore I don't feel guilty."

Vonda Maust, who lost 60 pounds through exercise and portion control, says, "I can't think of starting the day without my fitness workout, because it gets me energized for my busy day."

With the ball and bands, less really is more. You'll be able to see fast results in a minimum amount of time. Twelve moves in 12 minutes—it's that simple.

MORE CONVENIENCE PUTS YOU IN CONTROL

In addition to toning your entire body in just 12 minutes, you'll be able to exercise anywhere, anytime. The ball and bands also allow you more convenience and versatility than any other type of exercise equipment—and that convenience nearly guarantees that you'll keep your important commitment to yourself.

You can use the ball and bands to exercise in any room in your house. You can also easily toss them in a car for trips away from home. You can even deflate the ball and fit it and your bands into a suitcase for long-distance travel. Such convenience takes away all of the excuses that can get in the way of fitness. If your husband is watching a loud sports show, you have the option of taking your ball and bands upstairs to escape to a quieter spot for exercise. If you have small children, you can bring your ball and bands into their playroom and do your routine while you keep a watchful eye on them. On nice days, you can bring your equipment

> {"Convenience is the key to keeping up with your workout routine. The more convenient it is, the more likely you are to do it!"}

outside and work out with a cool breeze or in the sunshine. Staying motivated has never been easier.

HOW THE BALL AND BAND PROGRAM WORKS

The core of my ball and band program includes the following four crucial elements.

1. The "Daily Dozen" toning routine. On Mondays through Saturdays, you will spend about 12 minutes performing 12 efficient moves with the stability ball and bands. These Daily Dozen routines will tone and sculpt beautiful lean muscles in your legs, hips, tummy, arms, chest, and back. They will also improve your balance and coordination, your overall body strength, and your flexibility. At the end of each week, you will have sculpted and stretched all of your muscles, from head to toe.

2. A customized cardio plan. Cardiovascular (cardio) exercise helps condition your heart and lungs and burn fat. You will choose from five levels of cardio, based on your lifestyle and fitness goals.

3. A delicious eating plan. I often say that exercise is just one-half of the weight-loss equation. Nutrition is the other half.

My stability ball and band program includes 3 weeks of menus that focus on quick and easy meal options and recipes. I designed these menus with the help of Leslie Bonci, R.D., a registered dietitian who works with the country's top athletes. Each menu allows you to get the maximum enjoyment and satisfaction out of your food, while you spend the least amount of time possible in the kitchen and grocery store. Not even one meal will force you to drive all over town in search of a rare ingredient. Most meals contain just a handful of ingredients, take only 12 minutes to prepare, and taste fantastic. They are also wholesome, healthful, and great for trimming your waistline.

I've done all of the homework for you—you'll be eating about 1,500 calories a day and consuming the best types of foods to fuel weight loss—whole grains that give you the good-quality carbs your body needs for energy; healthy fats that make food taste yummy while boosting your mood, keeping your skin smooth and youthful, and helping your heart stay healthy; lean proteins that feed the muscle that will burn thousands of calories; and plenty of satisfying treats and snacks to keep you powered through those busy days!

4. Rejuvenating rest. During your 3-week plan in part 3, I've selected Sunday as the day for a very important fitness function: rest. Use your Sunday to revitalize yourself for the week to come, to let your muscles recover, and to recharge and refresh your mind. Each Sunday, you also will assess your progress by weighing in and taking your measurements. And because preparation is half the battle, I'll provide tips to help you get organized for the week ahead.

As you go through the book, you'll learn everything you need to know to successfully execute your program. In part 2, you'll find my favorite exercises and stretches using the ball and bands. For many of these exercises, I've included beginner, intermediate, and advanced versions, so you will always have options no matter what your fitness level. You'll also find a chapter that explains how you can mix and match these exercises into your own personalized program if you so choose.

In part 3, you'll find a day-by-day, 3-week plan that takes the best moves you learned in each of the workouts in part 2 and combines them into fun, unique, and challenging routines. Each day during your 3 weeks, you will find a 12-minute routine, a complete menu plan, a Daily Wisdom tip, and an inspiring story of how someone like you has lost weight and kept it off. You can always add more exercise to the mix if you like, but 12 minutes is your daily minimum requirement. Make this small commitment, and you'll feel *so* great!

LET'S TALK ABOUT PRIORITIES

Believe me, I know that you're busy. Maybe you have a full-time job, a family to feed, a house to clean, aging parents to look after, and countless other responsibilities. At times it may seem as if some things are more important than getting in your 12-minute routine. But in reality, nothing is more important than your health.

Even with the busiest schedule, it *is* possible to find time to exercise and eat right. I'm living proof. So how do I find time to exercise and eat right?

I don't. I *make* time.

I carve time out of my schedule for exercise, because my health is important to me.

Exercise and healthful eating will only become a priority for you once you make *you* your first priority. Think of your mind and body as you do your bank account. In your bank account, you must balance your expenditures with your deposits. Once you've taken care of food and shelter, you might give 10 percent of your earnings to charity, spend a large chunk on your children's education and their personal needs, and spend some more on special gifts to friends and family. But you know that you must deposit *more* than you withdraw; if you don't, your bank account eventually will become empty, and you will no longer be able to buy the gifts that bring joy to other people's lives.

It's the same with your mind and body. If you constantly donate your energy to taking care of others and neglect to make regular deposits to boost your internal reserves, your health will suffer and your energy will plummet. Rather than taking care of those you love, those you love will have to take care of you!

So don't feel selfish for depositing 12 minutes each day into your "internal bank account." It's 12 minutes that are well spent as an investment that will grow over time to produce dividends in health, fitness, and overall well-being. Your new healthy habits will rub off on those around you. I have two daughters, and I want to instill healthy habits in them, too. When I exercise, I exercise for me, for my daughters, and for my husband . . . and because I simply feel better afterward.

You can do it! I know you can. Believe in yourself. And before we move on, I'd like you to fill out the contract below, symbolically helping you to remember your commitment to yourself.

{ ## "Get fit, because you are worth it!" }

Once you've made your commitment, you can strengthen your motivation even further. Taking a "before" photo and keeping it in a visible place can help keep you focused on what's most important. Here are some additional motivational tips from fans who have lost weight and kept it off.

MY CONTRACT WITH MYSELF

I _____(write your name)_____ promise to create 12 minutes each day to improve my health and well-being.

I promise that I will:

▶ Make the most of the 12 minutes by completing my Daily Dozen routines

▶ Make time to exercise and not allow other distractions to get in the way

▶ Complete my Daily Dozen routine, no matter how busy my day

▶ Not feel guilty

Do mini workouts. I believe in what I call "fidgetcising," performing little movements all day that add up to big results. Paula Shupe, the woman I mentioned before who lost an amazing 42 pounds with exercise and healthful eating, suggests you "do 1 minute of exercise during every waking hour. This curbs the appetite, makes exercise *very routine*, and gives you a bonus of 15 minutes of toning every day."

Exercise at home. Lisa Flanagan, of West Seneca, New York, is the mother of a 3-year-old child and has recently lost 14 pounds. "I just can't take off like I used to, so I exercise at home," she says. "Sometimes I exercise early, sometimes later in the day, so I have the option of fitting it in when I have the time."

Inspire yourself with positive images. Tiffany Moore, a former model who lost 12 pounds with my exercise and healthful eating plan, told me that she has placed a photo of herself during her modeling days in front of her alarm clock. "I weighed 117½ pounds then, which was the perfect weight for my height," she says. "I never thought I'd be that size again, but I am. That photo gave me the motivation I needed to get out of bed in the mornings, instead of hitting the snooze button!"

Keep a food journal. Writing down what you eat and drink can help you stay on track. "I use the far right section of my daily planner each day to keep track of my food (approximate calories and grams of fat), water, vitamins, and exercise," says Sheila Stillman, who lost 60 pounds through my regular exercise and healthful eating plan. "I draw a heart in my journal for the days I exercise and write the type of exercise next to it. By the end of the week, there should be at least three hearts, completing a balanced workout schedule."

Mark it off. Write down on a calendar the workouts you plan to complete, including the type (toning, cardio, stretching) and length (12 minutes), suggests Laura Durava, who lost 29 pounds with regular exercise and healthful eating. "I draw a smiley face on my calendar for a good nutrition day and a sad face for days I fall off the wagon. I aim for 25 workouts a month and at least 20 smiley faces."

Focus on the intrinsic rewards. In addition to helping you shape up and lose weight, exercise boosts your mood, rids you of stress, and generally makes you feel good all over. "If I don't work out, I feel awful," says Dave Seguin, who lost a total of 147 pounds with my regular exercise plan and a healthful diet. "I put little reminders to myself on my computer at work. In my computer's Outlook calendar, I put a reminder notice that pops up when I log on to my e-mail. I also have added a new motivational tip to my screen saver every day. This has helped me a lot!"

Do it for your children. Getting fit does much more than help you look better. It also affects the health of your children. "If your children see an active mother, they will want to become active," says Karen Gaskill, who lost 49 pounds. "Your children imitate what they see, so if you live a healthy lifestyle, you are setting the best possible example you can for your children. You are helping to teach your children what it took so long for you to learn: Eating healthy and being fit are the keys to a successful body."

Give yourself feedback. In addition to stepping on the scale on a regular basis, I recommend that you find a symbolic way to measure your progress that also makes you feel good about yourself. For example, as she lost weight, Stephanie O'Reilly—who lost 50 pounds with my exercise plan and a healthful diet—tried on a snug old pair of shorts once a week. As the shorts grew more and more roomy, she became more and more motivated to stick to her program.

Persevere. Michelle Peace, who lost 25 pounds, summed it up best. "Don't give up when you don't see immediate results," she says. "You didn't get out of shape overnight, and you won't get in shape overnight either."

GET ON THE BALL

Once you've cemented your new priorities and decided how you will motivate yourself, you're ready to purchase your equipment. You're about to embark on a fun weight-loss system, one that will make you feel like a kid again. Turn to chapter 2 to find out everything you need to know about your equipment.

MIRACLE TOOLS

Why balls and bands get faster, stronger, better results

....
▼

Why do I feel so strongly that the stability ball and resistance bands are such vital fitness accessories for busy women and men? First and foremost, the research is clear—they are the most effective tools you can use to firm up and slim down. And the stability ball, in particular, has been shown in study after study to outperform the floor, chair, or weight bench as a workout aid.

For example, one recent study completed at Memorial University of Newfoundland in Canada and published in the *Journal of Strength and Conditioning Research* found that exercisers more effectively toned their muscles when they completed their sessions while seated on a stability ball compared to while seated on an exercise bench or chair. The unstable nature of the ball required the exercisers to use more effort to perform each movement. Another study published in the journal *Physical Therapy* and completed by researchers in Spain showed that exercisers recruited more muscle fibers in their abdomens to perform a curlup abdominal exercise on a ball versus on the floor. Other studies reveal similar results, showing that the ball makes every type of routine, from stretching to toning, more effective.

When you combine the stability ball with resistance bands, you are able to stretch and tone your muscles in any conceivable direction. This combination is good for your appearance *and* your health. For example, to keep your spine healthy, you must move it in all directions—forward, backward, to the sides, and in a twisting motion. Challenging your spine like this keeps it supple, healthy, and flexible. The same is true for the rest of your body. Other types of resistance only allow you to move linearly, toning just the front and back of your muscles. The resistance band and ball allow you to move your body in arcs and circles, toning the front, back, and *sides* of your muscles. You'll recruit more muscle fibers, tone a larger area of each muscle, and sculpt beautiful, firm curves throughout your body.

THE CORE WORKOUT

When you work out on the stability ball, you simultaneously tone the muscle you are targeting as well as your core—the group of muscles that form your abdomen, lower back, hips, and buttocks. For example, you'll feel many of the upper-body exercises not just in your chest, shoulders, or arms but also in your tummy, buttocks, and thighs.

For many of us, the tummy is the toughest spot to tone, because few exercises target all of the key muscles equally. Your abdomen is composed of three muscles.

- ▶ Your *rectus abdominis* forms the six-pack along the front of your abdomen that reaches from your sternum to your pelvic bone.

- ▶ Your *obliques* form the sides of your waistline.

- ▶ Your *transverse abdominis* lies underneath your rectus abdominis, supporting your back and holding in your belly.

Just sitting on the ball—without performing any official exercise—gives your body a workout. You will feel your obliques and your transverse abdominis firm as they work to stabilize your torso.

A strong transverse abdominis is the key to a flat tummy. When I work out on the ball, I can feel this deepest layer of my abdomen help me keep my balance. This critically important abdominal muscle goes unworked in many other forms of abdominal exercise, but my routines on the ball allow me to really feel it work and keep my abs in top shape.

Strengthening your transverse abdominis and other core muscles will do much more than flatten your tummy and shrink your waistline. A strong core supports your spine and holds your spine and pelvis in proper alignment. This helps improve your posture automatically and reduces lower-back pain.

Your core is also your power center, the part of your body where all movements originate. A strong core creates power in your midsection, helping you to accomplish fitness goals you would never have dreamed possible before. A strong core allows you to whack a tennis ball with more oomph, improve your golf swing, spring higher off a diving board, lift into a headstand or handstand, and perform just about any type of exercise with more ease. By working out with the ball and bands, you'll also develop the following:

Better posture. The stability ball forces you to maintain proper spinal alignment, making it very difficult to hurt yourself or "cheat" on a movement. It encourages your spine and the muscles around it to maintain alignment, which will improve your posture. You'll find that after only a week of using the ball, you'll be standing taller and feeling more balanced and centered on your feet. This change in your posture will make you look slimmer, even if you have lost only a small amount of weight on the scale.

Improved balance and coordination. Your balance can start to deteriorate in your forties as your muscles weaken and your nerve receptors lose sensitivity. The ball reverses this aging process by stabilizing your core. You'll work the small, deep muscles you use to keep your body steady while walking, and you'll also keep your spine supple and strong.

Well-rounded fitness. The curved surface of the ball and the flexible resistance of the bands allow you to perform stretching and toning moves with a greater range of motion, targeting every muscle from every angle and creating a long, lean, toned appearance. You can move your body in all directions, targeting your muscles like never before.

Less stress on your joints. Resistance bands work with your body's own resistance through the whole range of motion. The elasticity of the band allows you to stretch and relax it smoothly, preventing jerking that can damage muscles and injure joints. There's never any strain—key if you've experienced trouble with arthritis or chronic injury.

A fatter wallet! Your equipment will cost you less than $30 but will provide all of the benefits of a complete home gym. You can work every muscle group effectively, stretch, and even do your cardio workouts with your ball and bands.

A more convenient workout plan. Your ball and bands are easily stored, and neither takes up a lot of space or looks out of place in your living room—the colors can even complement your decor.

Also, the ball can deflate and fit in a suitcase, and the band easily fits in a handbag. Both are practically as light as air. I love to pack my bands into my suitcase or carry-on bag when I travel. During one long flight from Washington, D.C., to Los Angeles, I pulled my band out and did a series of stretches and other movements, getting in a mini workout on the airplane. How's that for time management?

Used together, these two portable, versatile, inexpensive, effective, and downright pretty tools can revolutionize your body!

BUYING YOUR EQUIPMENT

When you set out to get your new exercise tools, you'll find a wide variety of ball and band brands. You can purchase your equipment through my Web site (www.deniseaustin.com) or at sporting goods stores. No matter where you get your ball and bands, these pointers can help you get the best ones for you.

Get the right size. For proper body alignment, you need a ball that allows you to sit with your feet on the floor and knees bent at 90 degrees. If your knees bend more dramatically, your ball is too small. If the bend is less dramatic (larger than 90 degrees), your ball is too big. In general, the following chart should help you choose the right ball for your height.

BALL SIZES

Your Height	Ball Diameter
4'11"–5'4"	55 cm (21"–22")
5'5"–5'11"	65 cm (25"–26")
6'0" and up	75 cm (29"–30")

What if you already have a ball, but it's the wrong size? If your ball is too large, you can underinflate it. As you let the air out, keep checking to see when your knee hits that magic 90-degree angle. This strategy might work in the short term, but I recommend that you eventually buy a ball that is the right size. When you underinflate your ball, it won't move around as much underneath you and therefore won't challenge your balance as much—stealing one of the best benefits of ball workouts. If your ball is too small for you, give it to one of your children to use as a toy and buy yourself a larger ball.

Look for a burst-resistant ball. Some balls are designed to be "burst resistant."

This means that if something punctures your ball while you are sitting on it (such as a pin or a sharp toy), it will slowly lose pressure and not suddenly burst. (Remember the feeling you had, as a kid, of sitting on a balloon and having it pop? Trust me, you don't want that.)

Consider buying a pump. If you already have a bike pump, it will probably work just fine. A few manufacturers make small pumps designed specifically for inflating the ball. My ball comes packaged with one of these handy pumps. Most of these pumps are small enough to fit in a suitcase, allowing you to travel with your ball by deflating it and then inflating it once you reach your destination. They make pumping up your ball quick and easy.

Avoid balls with "feet." These balls look as if they have cow udders attached to one side. The feet help hold your ball in place when you are not using it. I don't recommend getting a ball with feet, because they will also hold the ball in place while you are on it, preventing the balancing challenge that makes exercising on the ball so effective.

Buy a variety of bands. Look for band packages that come with an easy- or light-resistance band, a medium-resistance band, and a heavy-resistance band. This will allow you to use lighter resistance for smaller muscles such as those in your arms and heavier resistance for larger muscles such as those in your back and chest. (See www.deniseaustin.com for a few bands that I love.)

Omit the fancy attachments. The best band is also the simplest. You need a band that is a few inches wide and a few feet long. I like mine because it's 5½ feet long—that's the best. You don't need handles, a stretch cord, or other fancy accoutrements.

CARING FOR YOUR EQUIPMENT

Your ball and bands require very little care, and if you take some extra precautions, you can help to extend their lives. With proper treatment, each of your new tools should last for years without breaking down.

Storage and Safekeeping

Store your ball and bands in a cool, dark place when possible. High temperatures and direct sunlight can wear down the latex and vinyl, causing your bands to rip and your ball to puncture more easily. Chlorine (from a swimming pool) will also reduce the life span of your equipment. When you're exercising, remove keys from your pockets, sharp jewelry, belt buckles, and anything else that could puncture the ball or rip your bands.

Also, keep your ball and bands away from your family pets. Just one bite from a large dog can deflate your ball for good.

Inflation

Follow these steps when you inflate your ball for the first time.

1. Some balls come with the air plug already in place. If so, remove it before you start to fill it with air.

2. Place the ball on the floor and smooth out any folds or wrinkles.

3. If you have a custom ball pump, insert the pump nozzle into the ball's air hole and start inflating. If your ball did not come with its own pump, it

INSPECT YOUR GADGETS

Both your resistance bands and ball should last years if you care for them properly. However, nothing lasts forever. The middle of your band—the part that you secure under your feet, hips, or back—will take the most abuse and will wear out first. Periodically examine it for small tears or cracks, and if you find any, replace it. If your ball seems chronically underinflated, it may have developed a small leak that allows air to escape slowly and silently. In this case, it's time to purchase a new ball.

▼

should come with an adapter that fits into most standard bike pumps. When using a bike pump or compressor, attach the ball adapter's threaded end to the bike pump or compressor. Then insert the needle into the ball and start pumping.

4. Fill the ball only until it is about 80 percent full. Let the ball sit overnight, allowing the air to settle and the ball to stretch.

5. In the morning, add more air as needed, filling the ball until it is firm. You should be able to press a finger into the ball and feel it give only slightly, about 2 to 3 inches.

Your ball is now ready for use! Every once in a while, take a good look at the ball to make sure it's still evenly inflated. Some balls can stretch over time, requiring more air.

Cleaning

If your ball and bands get dirty, rinse them and then air-dry them thoroughly. You can hang your bands from a drying rack, but not outside in the sun—as I mentioned, the sunlight will make them break down. Stay away from harsh chemicals, like cleaning products or water from a chlorinated swimming pool. If a harsh chemical gets on your ball and bands, wash them as soon as possible with tap water.

DESIGNING YOUR WORKOUT SPACE

Although balls and bands allow you to exercise anywhere, anytime, you'll definitely enjoy yourself more if you take care when planning your workout space. Chief among these considerations is giving yourself room to move! Make sure that you have enough freedom to move around without hitting furniture. The following pointers can help as well.

Complete your workouts on a smooth, nonslip surface. In the beginning, I suggest that you do your routines on a carpeted surface. This not only will feel more comfortable if you fall off the ball but also will steady the ball for you. After you've gotten more comfortable and confident, you can challenge yourself by moving your ball to a noncarpeted floor.

Avoid very hard surfaces. Particularly in the beginning, while you get used to the movements, steer clear of concrete and ceramic tile floors. You don't want to bump your head. A simple fall could become a bit more painful if it happens on a hard surface!

Use a mat. If you can't find a nonslip surface in your home, use an exercise or yoga mat under the ball to stabilize your feet.

YOUR CLOTHING

In most cases, the workout clothes that you already own will work just fine. You want to wear clothing that allows you to move freely and that doesn't bunch up. One caveat: Make sure you wear a top that covers your back and tummy. Exercising on the ball with just a sports bra will cause your skin to stick to the ball. This isn't dangerous, but it does feel uncomfortable.

In addition to wearing comfortable clothing, you may need to experiment with your hair, especially if it is long. A plastic hair clip will dig into the back of your head when you lie it against the ball or floor, so I recommend that you not use one. For most women with longer hair, a scrunchie or hair band will help keep hair out of the eyes and won't feel uncomfortable against the back of the head.

Because you won't be wielding heavy weights, you can safely exercise barefoot without worrying about dropping anything on your feet. Bare feet work just fine on most floor surfaces. If you find your feet slipping, however, definitely put on some shoes. Never work out while wearing socks, as your feet will slide out from under you.

WHAT TO EXPECT

When you first use your ball, you may feel a little awkward, silly, or even scared. Don't let those feelings deter you! I had given my sister Anne a stability ball, but she told me that she never used it. When I asked her why, she told me that she was scared to get on the ball. No matter how much I explained the ball's many benefits, she wouldn't try it. She said she was afraid that she would fall off.

One day while I was visiting her and the rest of my family in California, I made her sit on the ball. Then I made her lie on the ball. I spotted her by steadying her with my hands as she moved from one position to another. Eventually, I took a few steps back and watched as Anne balanced on the ball without my help. Now, she loves the ball and uses it on a regular basis. She has had three C-sections, and her ball workouts have made a real difference in the strength of her abs and back. They've also helped her to flatten her tummy.

No matter how fearful you are, no matter how awkward your first session, no matter how goofy you think you might look, trust that little by little, over time, you will get used to the new way of moving and you, too, will come to enjoy the stability ball as much as Anne and I do. To help reduce any apprehension that you might have about using the ball, take a moment to have a little fun and acquaint yourself with your new equipment. Rather than perform any "official" toning movements, just sit on your ball with your knees bent and both feet on the floor. If you feel wobbly, you can do this near a wall and place a hand on the wall for extra support.

Once you feel comfortable sitting on the ball, slowly bounce up and down. You don't need to make a big movement. Just bounce high enough to take yourself slightly off balance, as shown in the top photo on the opposite page. Never take your feet off the floor. As you bounce, pay attention to how your trunk and abdominal muscles respond. Feel them working to steady your body.

Once you feel comfortable with bouncing, sit still and lift one foot, as shown in the bottom photo. You don't need to lift it very high, just high enough that you feel your abdomen firm as it works to keep you balanced. Then lower that foot and lift the other one.

Next, try wiggling your hips around on the ball, as shown in the photo on page 26. Shift your hips back so that you feel a curve form in your lower spine and your body weight come forward on the backs of your thighs. Next, shift your hips forward, feeling your tailbone curl under. Then, try shifting them from the left to the right. Finally, move your hips in circles.

By now you should be starting to feel more comfortable on the ball. These other tips will also help you get started.

Feel the movement. For each exercise in this program, I've explained where you should feel the movement. For example, if an exercise says that it targets the backs of the legs, you'll want to focus on that area of your body, making sure you feel those muscles contracting as you move. As you focus inward and concentrate on the sensations in your muscles, you will tap into the internal wisdom of your body

Get comfortable on the ball by sitting and bouncing on it—soon it will be second nature!

Wiggling your hips on the ball will help you perfect your form.

and intuitively be able to optimize each exercise.

Have fun. If you lose your balance, laugh! Give yourself permission to have fun while your body learns this new skill. Each time you try it, your balance and coordination will improve.

Do a test run. If you feel intimidated by an exercise, break it down into slow movements. If the exercise combines the ball and band, omit the band during your trial run. Then, just bring your body into the basic position of the exercise. Hold for a few seconds and then come out of the position. For example, for the chest press (on page 86), forget the band at the beginning, and just bring your body into the shoulder bridge position. Then come out of it. Do this a few times. Once you feel comfortable, try it with the band.

EATING FOR PERFORMANCE

In general, you'll want to follow the same dietary advice for your ball and band routines that you would for any other type of workout. Certain positions require you to lie with your belly on the ball. If you've just eaten a large meal, this can feel uncomfortable. I recommend doing your ball routine first thing in the morning, when your stomach is empty. If you feel that you don't have enough energy, drink a glass of juice first or have a light snack. If you do your ball workout later in the day, make sure you do so at least 2 hours after eating.

Listen to your body and experiment with meal timing. Eventually, you'll discover the system that works best for you.

MAKE THE MOST OF YOUR EQUIPMENT

Your stability ball is probably the most versatile piece of exercise equipment you will ever purchase. Besides helping you get in an effective workout, it can also double as an office chair, a footrest, and a fun family toy.

Not long ago, I started using my stability ball as my office chair, and I noticed a change in my work style right away. Just sitting on the ball instead of in an office chair encouraged me to sit upright with proper posture, which helped keep my energy levels up as I completed paperwork or chatted on conference calls. I also find myself remembering to take mini stretch or workout breaks. After completing a task, I'll take 5 minutes to slide into a warrior pose (pages 156 and 158) or do a forward bend (page 166) on the ball. I find it fun and invigorating to shift my weight around and bounce every so often to keep the blood flowing.

If you decide to use your ball as your office chair, you may need to alter your desk configuration. You want your knees bent at a 90-degree angle when you sit on the ball. In certain situations, that may mean that your desk is too high. You can solve this problem by sitting on a larger ball and using a footrest (sold in office stores) to raise the level of your feet. Rest your feet flat on the floor or on your footrest. Keep your pelvis in a neutral position with a slight inward curve in your lower spine so that your sitting bones—not your tailbone—rest against the ball.

At first, sit on your ball for only 5 minutes or so. Then, slowly, work up to an hour and then 2 hours and then eventually all day. Sitting on the ball is a more active process than sitting in your desk chair, which means that your abdomen and back are constantly working to help you maintain an erect posture. You need to slowly train these muscles to hold you up. But if you do it slowly enough, you won't even realize you're "working out" while you sit and do your work!

As effective as the ball is, children should not sit on the ball when completing homework. Children are not tall enough to be able to sit on a ball and reach the level of a desk. On the other hand, try to encourage them to sit on a ball sized to their height when they watch television—they will have fun balancing and will give their bodies a challenge at the same time.

FUN WITH THE FAMILY

My two girls, Kelly and Katie, love the stability ball, too. They will do crunches on the ball along with me as well as various stretches. They *love* to challenge each other to balancing contests, doing the balancing stick (page 162), the plank (page 44), and other moves that you'll learn in coming chapters.

If you'd like to introduce your children to the ball, do so slowly in a controlled, safe environment. Make sure sharp objects and furniture are out of the way.

For your small toddler, try draping him over the ball and steadying his back with one hand. Also, try sitting across from a small child, rolling the ball to her, and seeing if she will roll it back. Older children can safely do most of the balancing and stretching exercises suggested in this book; however, I don't recommend teaching them the toning exercises with the band. Use the ball to energize them about fitness and show them that fitness can indeed be *fun*. Let them exercise without knowing they are doing it.

BLAST OFF TO YOUR BEST BODY

Now that you know everything you need about purchasing, caring for, and familiarizing yourself with your equipment, you're ready to learn my favorite ball and band exercises. Remember: Give yourself permission to feel awkward. Give yourself permission to laugh. Give yourself permission to spend time focusing on *you!*

Turn to part 2 and find the best and most effective ball and band exercises for sculpting your entire body. Have a ball!

PART 2

THE BALL AND BAND BASICS

ch.

(3)

SCULPTING YOUR CORE MUSCLES

Trim your waistline, flatten your belly, and lose those love handles

I love toning my tummy with the ball. I have to do only a few repetitions of any of these 16 core exercises and I really feel it. No matter what part of my body I'm targeting, I'm *always* sculpting my core muscles—my abs, back, waist, hips, and butt—as they work to keep me balanced.

In addition to the core strength I get from balancing on the ball, I also do a series of very specific exercises that zero in on crucial midsection areas, working my abs, back, and sides from every angle. In this chapter, I'm going to share those exercises with you. Do them twice a week or more, and you will love the results!

If you look in the mirror and think, "Boy, my body needs a good dose of middle management," keep in mind that tummy flab could be the result of many things. First, simple lack of use allows your internal organs to press against your abdominal wall, creating a rounded appearance, even if you carry no extra fat in your abdomen. Second, pregnancy and menopause also can weaken your

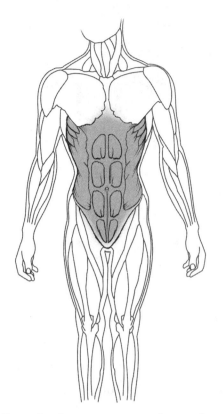

Strengthening your core muscles can flatten your tummy and help you stand taller.

midsection. As a baby grows in the womb, the surrounding abdominal muscles stretch outward. If you don't tighten up those muscles after delivery, your abs will remain loose and weak. And third, and probably least fair of all, some people are just genetically predisposed to store fat in their midsections.

To turn things around, however, you need to spend about 12 minutes, 2 or 3 days a week, to whip your abdomen into shape. The exercises in this chapter will help you to target five specific core muscles.

▶ **Your upper and lower rectus abdominis.** Fibrous bands of tissue break up this large muscle that runs from your pubic bone to your ribs along the front center of your abdomen, creating the six-pack appearance. Though the rectus abdominis really is one large muscle, I like to think of it as two distinct ones—one below the navel and one above it—since you must perform one type of exercise to tone the upper area and another exercise to tone the lower section of the rectus abdominis.

▶ **Your transverse abdominis.** The ball can really help tone this muscle. This deepest layer of the abdomen lies underneath your rectus abdominis and helps you contract your abdomen and draw your belly inward. Strengthening it creates a natural girdle for the front and sides of your midsection.

▶ **Your obliques.** Internal and external obliques form your sides and waist. Your external obliques sit closest to the surface toward the front of your waist, with the internal obliques sitting deeper and closer to your back. Toning them shrinks your waistline and love handles.

▶ **Your lower back.** Your lower back contains numerous muscles. One group, called the erector spinae, attaches to your spinal column at different points along your back, allowing you to bend it forward and backward and from side to side. Toning these muscles helps prevent back pain, and it also tightens and firms your entire lower back. That's handy for shrinking love handles or any other back flab that may stick out over your bikini, underwear, or low-rider jeans.

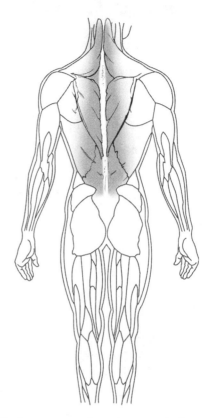

Toning your erector spinae can help relieve back pain.

The following pages show 16 stability ball exercises that zero in on the core muscles. When doing each exercise, pay careful attention to your body alignment. A few repetitions of an exercise done correctly—to completely work your abdomen—are better than 20 sloppy ones. Remember quality over quantity.

For most exercises, perform up to 12 repetitions. In a few of the movements, you'll simply hold the posture up to 1 minute. When multiple variations of an exercise are shown, try the initial, beginner version first and then progress to the intermediate variation when you feel ready.

Some of these exercises are very challenging, but don't let that discourage you! In the 3-week plan in part 3, I start you off slowly with beginner exercises during week 1 and gradually build up to intermediate and advanced moves by week 3.

PELVIC TILT

▶ **Firms your lower belly**

▶ **Stretches your lower back**

This is a great warmup exercise. I like to do it at the beginning of an abdominal routine to ready my abs for harder movements.

A. Sit on the ball with your knees bent and feet on the floor. Extend your arms in front of you at shoulder height.

B. Exhale as you tuck your tailbone in, activate your abs, and bring your navel in toward your spine. Inhale as you release the tilt in your pelvis. Repeat tucking and releasing 12 times.

BACK STRETCH

- ► **Opens your chest**
- ► **Relaxes your abdomen**
- ► **Elongates your spine**

I like to do this stretch periodically during my abdominal routines to give my tummy a little break.

A. Sit on the ball with your knees bent and feet on the floor. Walk your feet forward as you slide your torso down the ball until your lower and mid back press into the ball, as shown. Exhale as you raise your arms overhead.

B. Continue to exhale as you lean back over the ball, allowing the ball to support the arch in your spine. Reach your fingertips toward the floor and fully extend your legs, as shown. Then inhale as you return to the starting position, lying back on the ball with your arms down. Stretch back over the ball two more times.

TRADITIONAL CRUNCH

► **Firms your upper- and lower-tummy areas**

If you've done any exercises on the ball before, this is probably one of the first move-ments you learned. The ball allows you to crunch against more resistance and through a greater range of motion than you would on the floor—but only if you do it correctly. It pays to zero in closely on your posture. A few small tweaks allow you to completely fa-tigue your abdomen in just a few repetitions, saving you lots of time!

A. Sit on the ball with your knees bent and feet on the floor. Walk your feet forward as you slide your torso down the ball only until your hips start to clear the ball and the very bottom of your lower back presses into the ball. Cross your arms over your chest.

Now here's where you really need to focus on your posture. Lie back on the ball so that your upper back also rests against the ball, as shown. Then tuck your tailbone in and lift your hips toward the ceiling. You should already feel your lower tummy and buttocks firm in this position— and you haven't performed a single crunch!

B. Exhale as you lift your torso, pull your navel in, and contract your abdomen. Imagine you are curling the bottom of your rib cage and your pelvic bone toward each other, creating a firm arc with your lower body. Keep your chin up, as if you were holding an orange between your chin and neck. Inhale as you return to the starting position, lying all the way back on the ball. Do as many repetitions as you can, up to a total of 12.

Intermediate Crunch

C. To increase the challenge, interlace your fingers behind your head with your elbows out to the sides. This will add some weight to your upper body, creating more resistance for you to work against. As you crunch in this position, keep your elbows out to the sides (you should not be able to see them) and avoid using your hands to assist.

Advanced Crunch

D. To increase your resistance even more, extend your arms overhead with your palms together.

Super Crunch

E. With your hands behind your head, lift and extend one leg as you crunch. This will put you off balance, forcing muscles in your legs and core to shift and firm to steady you.

OBLIQUE TWIST

▶ **Trims the sides of your abdomen**

▶ **Shrinks your waistline**

As with the traditional crunch, proper posture is key to reaping the maximum effectiveness of the ball.

A. Sit on the ball with your knees bent and feet on the floor. Walk your feet forward as you slide your torso down the ball until your lower back presses into the ball. Come into the crunch position, as described in the traditional crunch on page 36.

Place your right palm behind your head with your elbow out to the side, and place the palm of your left hand on your lower belly, as shown. Tuck your tailbone in and reach up through your hips.

B. Exhale as you lift and twist your torso, bringing your right shoulder toward your left knee. Keep your tailbone tucked in throughout. You should feel the muscles in your lower belly firm as they work to stabilize you. Inhale as you return to the starting position. Repeat lifting and lowering for up to 12 repetitions. Then switch sides.

Advanced Oblique Twist

C. Lifting one leg will put you off balance, making muscles throughout your body work harder to hold you steady. Get into the crunch position, as described in the beginner version. As you crunch up, lift your opposite knee toward your opposite shoulder. As you release the crunch, lower your leg to the floor.

{ "Nothing works your tummy
like being on the ball!" }

TORSO TONER

▶ **Strengthens your core muscles**

▶ **Firms your thighs and buttocks**

Now, here's an exercise that wouldn't exist if it weren't for the ball. The ball's round surface allows you to rotate your torso from one side to the other, strengthening the deepest core muscles. You'll feel everything from your feet to your shoulders working to steady you on this one!

A. Lie with your upper back, shoulders, and head on the ball. Your knees should be bent at 90-degree angles with your feet on the floor, a hip's distance apart or wider. Extend your arms from your chest and press your palms together. Squeeze your knees together. Hold for 30 seconds as you breathe deeply.

Intermediate Torso Toner

B. Once you can balance for 30 seconds in the beginner version, you're ready to rotate from side to side. Exhale as you bring your arms to the left and lift your right shoulder off the ball, as if you were swinging a bat. Inhale as you return to the starting position. Exhale as you "swing your bat" to the right. Continue to alternate sides up to 12 times.

LOWER-TUMMY FIRMER

▶ **Firms and flattens your lower belly**

▶ **Tones your inner thighs**

I love this exercise because it is so effective for both the lower tummy and the inner thighs, working below the belly button.

A. Lie on your back with your arms down near your sides, palms facing down. Grasp the ball between your feet with your legs extended at a 90-degree angle to your torso. You'll really feel it in your inner thighs.

B. Exhale as you curl your lower belly toward your upper belly, lifting the ball up and in. Inhale as you lower. Continue to lift and lower the ball up to 12 times.

TUMMY FLATTENER

▶ Firms your entire tummy

This is a great crunch position for beginners who lack the abdominal strength for the traditional crunch on top of the ball.

A. Lie on your back with your knees bent and heels on the ball. Extend your arms toward your knees.

B. Exhale as you lift your shoulders up toward the ball. The ball will shift and move slightly, forcing you to use your leg muscles to keep it from rolling away. Inhale as you lower. Repeat up to 12 times.

WAISTLINE TRIMMER

▶ **Firms the sides of your tummy**

▶ **Shrinks your waistline**

As with the tummy flattener, this is a great option for beginners who lack the abdominal strength for the oblique twist.

A. Lie on your back with your knees bent and heels on the ball. Interlace your fingers behind your head with your elbows out to the sides.

B. Exhale as you lift your left shoulder toward your right hip. The ball will shift and move slightly, forcing you to use your leg muscles to keep it from rolling away. Inhale as you lower. Then lift your right shoulder toward your left hip. Repeat up to 12 times.

PLANK

- ▶ **Strengthens your core muscles**
- ▶ **Improves balance and coordination**
- ▶ **Tones your upper body**

In this exercise the ball will shift under your body weight, causing your abdominal and leg muscles to firm as they steady you. You will feel the deepest layer of your abdomen working. This is what will help keep your abs flat.

A. Kneel with the ball about 1 foot in front of you. Place your forearms on top of the ball with your palms together and fingers interlaced. Pull your navel up and in. Contract and "zip up" your abs.

B. Exhale as you lift your knees and extend your legs, balancing on the balls of your feet and your forearms. The closer together your legs, the harder it will be to balance. Hold for up to 1 minute as you breathe normally.

Advanced Plank

C. To firm your upper body and completely tone your core muscles, try lifting your palms and balancing on the backs of your upper arms. Keep your back straight and your abs tight.

{ *"'Zip up' your abs—anytime, anywhere!"* }

NATURAL TUMMY TUCK

▶ **Strengthens your core muscles**

▶ **Improves balance and coordination**

▶ **Tones your upper body**

This challenging move can really boost your metabolism. It targets your transverse abdominis muscle, to retrain your tummy muscles.

A. Start in a pushup position with your shins on the ball and your hands on the floor under your chest. (*Note:* Positioning the ball so that your thighs are against it makes the exercise easier.) Firm your abdominals and lift your hips so that your back is flat.

B. Exhale as you tuck your knees in toward your chest, moving the ball along the floor as you do so. Inhale as you return to the starting position. Continue to tuck and then uncoil up to 12 times.

ULTIMATE TUMMY TRIMMER

Flattens your tummy below the waistline

The flexible resistance of the band will make your torso work harder to remain stable in this exercise.

A. Lie on your back with your knees bent and feet on the floor. Lift your feet toward the ceiling and place the middle of the resistance band across your arches. Hold the ends of the band with your hands. Form a 90-degree angle between your legs and torso. Lift your upper body until your shoulder blades hover just above the surface of the floor, as shown.

B. Exhale as you slowly lower your legs. Keep your hands stationary, stretching the band. Stop once you can no longer keep your spine against the floor. Inhale as you rise to the starting position. Repeat up to 12 times.

BICYCLE

- ▶ **Firms your lower tummy**
- ▶ **Improves spine stability**

Similar to the single-leg stretch in Pilates, this exercise zeros in on the lower tummy as you lengthen your legs away from your torso.

A. Lie on your back with your knees bent and feet on the floor. Hold the ball above your chest. Lift your feet and bring your knees in toward your chest. Exhale as you extend your right leg. Pull your belly button in and tighten your abs.

B. Inhale as you bring your right leg in to your chest and simultaneously extend your left leg. Keep your lower spine against the floor and the ball motionless as you move. Repeat up to 12 times.

Intermediate Bicycle

C. Lift your head and shoulders to help you simultaneously target your upper- and lower-tummy areas.

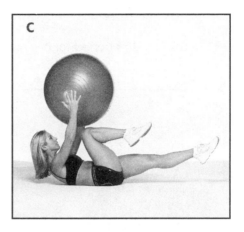

{ *"This variation on a classic is updated with the ball."* }

BACK TONER

► **Strengthens your lower back**

The back toner is perfect for beginners with weak back muscles.

A. Lie with your tummy on the ball, your knees bent, and your shins against the floor. Interlace your fingers behind your head with your elbows out to the sides.

B. Exhale as you lift your head, arms, and upper torso toward the ceiling. Stop rising when your spine is flat. Inhale as you return to the starting position. Repeat up to 12 times.

LOWER-BACK STRENGTHENER

▶ **Strengthens your lower back**

▶ **Improves coordination**

As you lift and lower your legs during this exercise, the ball will shift under your tummy, forcing your ab muscles to work hard to stabilize your torso. Tighten your abs and pull your navel in and up toward your spine.

A. Lie with your tummy on the ball. Extend both arms and place both hands against the floor. Extend both legs behind, balancing on the balls of your feet.

B. Exhale as you lift your left leg as high as you can. Inhale as you lower it. Repeat with your right leg. Try to keep your torso stable as you lift and lower each leg, to prevent any wobbling. Continue to alternate legs for 12 repetitions on each side.

RISE AND SHINE

▶ **Strengthens your lower back**

Similar to the back toner, the rise and shine takes back strengthening to the next level. The curved surface of the ball helps keep your pelvis in the ideal position for back bends, reducing strain to the joints in your lower spine.

A. Lie with your tummy on the ball, your knees bent, and your shins against the floor. Rest your palms on the floor in front of the ball with your arms in a wide angle.

Exhale as you lift your head, arms, and upper torso toward the ceiling, as shown. Squeeze your buttocks muscles at the top of the motion. Inhale as you return to the starting position. Repeat up to 12 times.

Intermediate Rise and Shine

B. Extending your legs behind will challenge your balance as you lift and lower your torso.

Advanced Rise and Shine

C. Placing your feet against the wall and your hands behind your head will help you to lift just a bit higher.

{ "Protect and strengthen your back with this fun exercise." }

RECIPROCAL REACH

▶ **Strengthens your lower back**

▶ **Improves coordination**

You may have done reciprocal reaches without the ball during one of my videos or my TV show. Doing them on the ball helps keep your pelvis properly aligned, preventing the lower back from arching. It also will challenge your balance as you lift and reach with your opposite arm and leg.

A. Lie with your tummy on the ball. Extend your legs and rest the balls of your feet against the floor. Extend both arms and place both palms against the floor, under your chest.

B. Exhale as you lift and extend your right arm and left leg. Inhale as you lower them. Exhale as you lift and extend your left arm and right leg. Inhale as you lower them. Continue to alternate sides for 12 repetitions on each side.

ch.
④
.......▶

SCULPTING YOUR LOWER BODY

Slim your thighs, lift your buttocks, and shrink your hips

▾

My personal trouble spot is my thighs. When I snack a little too much or slack off on my fitness routine, I definitely see it in my thighs. Fortunately, the ball and bands have allowed me to fit in quick and effective routines that target muscles in my lower half from every angle, helping to shape and firm my thighs in a minimum amount of time.

My 19 favorite lower-body moves will help you to lift your buttocks, slim your hips and thighs, and firm and shape your entire lower half. Try these exercises, and you'll soon make your lower half your better half! To understand how the ball and band exercises in this chapter work, let's first take a look at the anatomy and physiology of your bottom half.

If your lower half is currently *not* your better half, the culprit may be a combination of several factors. Most often, it's due to genetics. Some of us—myself included—have inherited a set of genes that directs the cells in our bodies to deposit excess fat on our hips, thighs, and buttocks. We gain weight in this area first and lose it here last. To turn things around, we must target the following specific areas of the lower body.

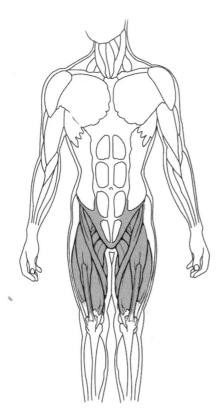

Sculpt beautiful, lean, and long legs with ball and band exercises that focus on your adductors, abductors, quadriceps, and hip flexors.

▸ **Inner thighs.** Numerous muscles along your inner thighs work together to stabilize your knees and hips as you walk. Collectively, these muscles are known as your adductors. They include the adductor magnus, minimus, longus, and brevis. Toning these muscles will help prevent your inner thighs from jiggling or rubbing when you walk.

▸ **Outer thighs and hips.** The muscles that help you do the standard leg lift are called your abductors, and they include the gluteus medius and minimus along your hips. Toning these muscles helps you smooth away saddlebags. It also helps to draw them inward, creating sexy indentations in your outer hips.

▸ **Front thighs.** The muscles that form the fronts of your thighs include your quadriceps, a series of four muscles that help you to extend your knee and lift your leg. Near the top of the front of your thighs is another series of small muscles collectively called your hip flexors (the psoas major, psoas minor, and iliacus), which also help you lift your leg as well as propel your leg forward when you walk or climb stairs.

▸ **Rear thighs.** Your hamstrings form the backs of your thighs, from your

knees to your buttocks. Toning these
muscles creates a great rear view and
helps prevent cellulite.

▶ **Buttocks.** Collectively called your
gluteals (glutes), your buttocks are
formed by your gluteus minimus,
medius, and maximus. You will firm
these muscles and shape and lift your
buns.

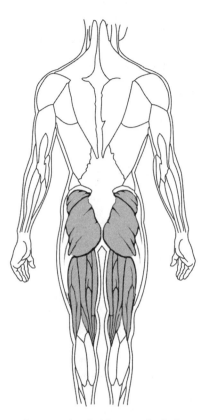

The following 19 exercises target those important lower-body areas. You'll notice that I've
included the band strategically in a few exercises, where it can really help you to target
your lower body.

Perform up to 12 repetitions of each exercise. In a few movements, you'll simply hold
the posture up to 1 minute. When multiple
variations of an exercise are shown, try the initial, beginner version first. Also, as I mentioned

Toning your backside—particularly your
hamstrings and gluteals—helps prevent
cellulite.

with the abdominal exercises, some of these exercises can be challenging at first,
but don't let that stop you! During your 3-week plan in part 3, I start you off
slowly with beginner exercises during week 1 and gradually build up to intermediate and advanced moves by week 3.

THIGH BLASTER

► **Tones your buttocks**

► **Firms the backs of your thighs**

Similar to a squat that you might do at the gym, the thigh blaster allows you to roll up and down on the ball, protecting your knees. The band adds extra resistance, making the exercise more effective.

A. Sit on the ball with your knees bent and feet on the floor. Walk your feet forward as you slide down the ball, until your lower back rests against the ball, as shown. Your feet should be far enough away from the ball for your thighs to be parallel with the floor. Secure the band under your feet and grasp an end of the band in each hand with your hands by your hips.

B. Exhale as you straighten your legs. Inhale as you return to the starting position. Repeat 12 times.

Intermediate Thigh Blaster

C. Doing the thigh blaster with one leg extended increases the challenge to the working leg and makes your core muscles work harder to keep you balanced. Start in the same position as for the thigh blaster, but secure the band under just one foot, raising and extending the other. Do up to six repetitions on one leg and then switch legs.

{ "Get right at that upper-thigh zone without killing your knees!" }

WALL SQUAT

Tones your thighs and buttocks

Placing a ball between your back and the wall makes this exercise easier on the knees. It also makes you work harder to stay balanced. This will reshape your legs and buttocks quickly—you'll really feel it!

A. Stand with your ball between your lower back and a wall or a closed door. Inch your feet away from the wall so that your body weight leans into the wall and your feet are about 1 to 1½ feet in front of your hips, as shown. Cross your arms over your chest.

B. Inhale as you bend your knees and slide your back and ball down the wall, keeping constant pressure between your back and the ball. Once your knees bend 90 degrees, as shown, exhale as you rise to the starting position. Repeat up to 12 times.

Note: If your knees reach past your toes, your feet are too close to the wall. Inch your feet out farther until your knees are directly over your ankles when bent at 90 degrees.

Intermediate Wall Squat

C. Securing a band under your feet will increase the resistance to tone your legs as you squat up and down. It will also strengthen your upper body. Grasp an end of the band in each hand, bending your elbows and bringing your hands near shoulder level. Keep your hands in this position as you squat down and up. Keep your abs tight and engaged.

{ "For extra results, on your last rep hold in the down position, place a soccer ball between your knees, and squeeze it. Hold for as long as you can and then release. You can do it!" }

BALL TAP

▶ **Improves coordination and balance**

▶ **Tones your thighs and buttocks**

This exercise requires a certain amount of trust. Just give it a try, but if you feel wary of this exercise, try it first on carpeting (which will help hold the ball steady) or with the ball against a wall.

A. Stand with your feet slightly wider than your hips. Place your ball about 1 foot behind your lower legs. Cross your arms over your chest (this will prevent you from using your arms to create momentum on the way up).

B. Inhale, bend your knees, and sit back onto the ball. As soon as your hips touch the ball, exhale and rise to the starting position, as if the ball were too hot to sit upon. Do this slowly at first. As you get used to the motion, you can move more quickly. Repeat up to 12 times.

FLOOR TAP

► **Tones your thighs and core muscles**

► **Improves balance and coordination**

This challenging exercise is great for those of you who ski or play sports that require you to constantly shift your body weight. Be gentle with yourself and have some fun. Your balance will improve over time.

A. Stand on your right foot. Bend your left leg and lift your left foot off the floor. Hold the ball with your arms extended in front of you. Engage your abs.

B. Inhale as you bend forward and bring the ball toward the floor. Just as the ball taps the floor, exhale as you return to the starting position. Repeat up to six times and then switch legs.

HAMSTRING CURL

▶ **Firms the backs of your thighs**

▶ **Reshapes your bottom half**

Hamstring curls are a perfect complement to the bottoms-up (on page 66). I like to do them one after another in my routines.

A. Lie on your back with your knees bent and feet against the ball. Rest your arms at your sides with your palms facing down. Exhale as you lift your hips and back off the floor, as shown, balancing on your upper back and heels.

B. Inhale as you bend your knees and pull the ball toward your hips. Exhale as you extend your legs. Continue to extend and curl the ball 12 times.

Intermediate Hamstring Curl

C. Technically called the hip curl, this slight variation packs a big punch and will help zero in on and lift your buns. Start with your heels on the ball and shoulders and upper back on the floor. As you bend your knees and bring the ball in toward your hips, simultaneously lift your hips and torso, as shown, rising until only your shoulders touch the floor.

BOTTOMS-UP

► **Firms the backs of your thighs and your buttocks**

► **Strengthens your abdomen**

I love this exercise because it really tones and shapes my legs. I don't have to dig my heels into the ball for very long before I feel it, right where I need it.

A. Lie with your back on the floor and your arms down at your sides, about 45 degrees away from your torso, palms facing down. Rest your heels and calves on top of the ball.

Exhale as you raise your hips toward the ceiling and balance on the backs of your shoulders and your heels, as shown. Squeeze your thighs together and dig your heels into the ball. Do you feel it? Hold for 30 to 60 seconds, as you breathe normally, and then release.

Advanced Bottoms-Up

B. To *really* feel it, try this exercise with only one leg on the ball. Extend the other leg toward the ceiling.

BALL SQUEEZE

▶ **Firms your inner thighs**

▶ **Strengthens your lower belly**

This exercise is so simple, yet so effective.

A. Lie on your back with your arms down at your sides, palms facing down. Inhale and grasp the ball between your calves with your legs extended. Lift the ball off the floor as you exhale. Squeeze the ball between your legs as hard as you can, pulsing so that you alternate between squeezing and releasing, squeezing and releasing for 20 to 30 seconds, as you breathe normally, and then release.

Advanced Ball Squeeze

B. Adding a twist to the ball squeeze will tone your lower belly and improve your coordination. Exhale as you squeeze your legs into the ball and rotate your feet clockwise. Inhale as you return to the starting position. Then rotate counterclockwise. Continue rotating the ball left and right, bringing your feet in a semicircular motion, for 20 to 30 seconds.

LOWER-BODY TONER

▶ **Improves balance and coordination**

▶ **Strengthens all of your core muscles**

▶ **Tones your buttocks and outer thighs**

This challenging exercise can be a lot of fun if you give yourself permission to laugh at your foibles.

A. Lie on your back with your feet and calves against the ball, about 1 foot apart from each other. Rest your arms at your sides with your palms facing down. Exhale as you lift your hips and back off the floor, balancing on your shoulders and heels. Bring your feet toward the floor to the left, as shown, rolling the ball to the left as you do so. Go as far as you can without losing your balance.

B. Inhale as you return to center and exhale as you repeat to the right. Continue alternating left and right for up to 12 total repetitions.

OUTER-THIGH TONER

▶ **Shrinks saddlebags**

▶ **Strengthens your arms**

When you lean your upper body against the ball to do the traditional leg lift, you get two workouts in one. Your upper body will strengthen as it supports and balances your body weight against the ball. The sides of your waist get a workout, too.

A. Kneel with the ball to your left side. Lean your left side into the ball and rest your left forearm on top of the ball for balance. Extend your right leg. Pull your navel in and contract your abs.

B. Exhale as you lift your right leg as high as you can. Inhale as you lower it. Repeat 12 times and then switch sides.

BUTT AND THIGH FIRMER

► **Tones and lifts your buttocks**

► **Firms the backs of your thighs**

► **Strengthens your arms**

As with the outer-thigh toner, you'll get two workouts in one as you lean your upper body into the ball.

A. Kneel with the ball in front of you. Lean forward and place your forearms onto the ball. Extend your right leg behind your torso, as shown. Pull your navel in and engage your abs.

B. Exhale as you lift your extended leg as high as you can without arching your back. Inhale as you lower it. Repeat up to 12 times and then switch legs.

DEADLIFT

- ▶ **Strengthens all of your core muscles**
- ▶ **Lifts your buttocks and lengthens your legs**
- ▶ **Improves your balance**

The ball allows you to do a traditional deadlift without hurting your knees.

A. Stand while holding the ball with your arms extended at chest level. Shift your body weight onto your right foot and extend your left foot behind your torso.

B. Inhale as you bend forward, extend your left leg behind and up, and touch the ball against the floor. Exhale as you rise to the starting position. Repeat up to 12 times and then switch legs.

LUNGE

► **Tones your hips, thighs, and buttocks**

► **Improves balance and coordination**

Adding the ball to the traditional lunge helps you work a greater proportion of muscle fibers in your thighs as the ball puts you off balance.

A. Stand with the ball to your right side. Rest your right hand on top of the ball. Take a large step forward with your left leg.

B. Inhale as you bend your left knee and sink down into the lunge. Exhale as you rise to the starting position. Repeat up to 12 times and then switch sides.

LEG LUNGE

- ▶ **Firms your thighs and buttocks**
- ▶ **Works your abdomen**
- ▶ **Strenghthens your feet and ankles**

Performing the lunge with your rear foot on the ball increases the challenge to your balance.

A. Stand with your left shin on the ball and your hands on your hips.

B. Inhale as you bend your right leg and reach back through your left leg, extending your left leg as you move the ball along the floor. Exhale as you rise to the starting position. Repeat up to 12 times and then switch legs.

BACK-OF-THIGH TONER

▶ **Lifts your buttocks**

▶ **Firms the backs of your thighs**

▶ **Strengthens your arms, back, and abdomen**

I was doing deadlifts with my ball one day when suddenly I had the idea for this exercise. Once I tried it, I loved it. This little gem tones just about every muscle in your body.

A. Stand while holding the ball with your arms extended at chest level. Shift your body weight into your right foot and extend your left foot behind your torso. Bend forward and place the ball against the floor, as shown. Keep your abs engaged.

B. Exhale as you raise your left leg and then inhale as you lower it toward the floor. Try to keep your hips level as you move. Repeat up to 12 times and then switch legs.

Intermediate Back-of-Thigh Toner

C. Simply bending your rear leg and lifting your foot toward the ceiling will help to zero in on that little bundle of fat that tends to bulge from the bottom of your swimsuit.

{ "When you work with the ball, a few simple movements can get you great results!" }

QUAD SETS

► **Tone the fronts of your thighs**

This exercise is deceptively more challenging than it appears.

A. Sit on the ball with your knees bent and feet on the floor. Place your palms against the ball for balance. "Zip up" your abs.

B. Shift your weight onto your right foot. Exhale as you lift your left knee as high as you can without losing your balance. Keep your lower back straight as you do so. Don't allow it to arch outward. Hold for 30 seconds, breathing normally, and then release and repeat with the other leg. If you lose your balance before 30 seconds, just put your foot down, reestablish your balance, and try again.

Intermediate Quad Sets

C. Once you can easily keep your balance with your knee bent, try it with your leg extended and hands behind your head. Don't allow your torso to wobble or your lower back to arch outward. Keep your abs tight.

{ *"Give yourself permission to sometimes take your time—balance is all about patience."* }

THIGH SHAPER

▶ **Firms your inner and outer thighs**

▶ **Strengthens your core muscles**

▶ **Lifts your buns**

This exercise is extremely challenging but worth every bit of effort. If you experience trouble balancing on the ball, have a little faith. The more you try it, the better your balance will become.

A. Stand with one side of your body near a wall and the ball just in front of you. Kneel into the ball and place one palm on top of the ball and the other palm against the wall for support.

Lift your feet and roll forward on the ball until your shins are on top of the ball. Flex your feet and press the tops of your feet against the side of the ball. Lift your torso, as shown. Try to balance in this position for up to 1 minute, taking your hand away from the wall and putting it back against the wall as needed when you feel yourself losing your balance. Remember to breathe. Squeeze your inner thighs to help position yourself. Keep your abs tight.

Advanced Thigh Shaper

B. As you become more proficient at the thigh shaper, try it without using the wall for support. First, kneel on the ball with your palms and knees against the ball, as shown. As you gain your balance, lift your torso and arms and balance with only your knees and shins against the ball.

{ *"This move is tough, but it sometimes reminds me of being a kid in gym class!"* }

HIP SLIMMER

► **Shrinks saddlebags**

► **Slims your outer thighs and hips**

You need only the band for this exercise to really target those outer thighs.

A. Secure the band under your feet and stand with your feet under your hips. Grasp the ends of the band with both hands and position your hands by your navel.

B. Exhale as you lift your extended left leg out to the side as high as you can. Inhale as you return to the starting position. Repeat on the other side. Continue to alternate sides for 12 total repetitions on each side.

INNER-THIGH SHAPER

Firms your inner thighs

I love this exercise. It's one of the best ways to firm up your inner thighs. You'll simultaneously firm your standing leg as well as the one pressing into the band. Did you know that your inner thigh has one of the most underused muscles of the body? But this exercise targets *right there.*

A. Stand with the band secured under your left foot. Grasp an end of the band in each hand and gather up the excess until the band is taut. Lift your right leg slightly, bringing the inner edge of your right foot against the band.

B. Cross the band in front of you. Exhale as you press your right foot into the band and bring it to the left. Inhale as you return to the starting position. Repeat up to 12 times and then switch legs.

LEG CIRCLES WITH BAND

▶ **Firm your inner and outer thighs**

▶ **Strengthen your abdomen**

This exercise originates from the Pilates method. Adding the band really helps to target your legs and make smooth circles. It also encourages proper body alignment.

A. Lie on your back with your left leg extended on the mat and your right leg lifted toward the ceiling, with the exercise band wrapped around the arch of your right foot. Hold both ends of the band in your right hand at chest level with your elbow bent. Extend your left arm out to the side for balance. Engage your abs.

B. Slowly circle your right foot counterclockwise, dipping down to the floor as you move your foot around the circle. Make four large circles— exhaling as you lower your leg and inhaling as you raise your leg—and then switch direction, circling clockwise. Then switch legs and repeat.

5

SCULPTING YOUR UPPER BODY

Shape sexy arm, shoulder, and back muscles

Combine the smooth, yet constant, resistance of the band with the instability of the ball, and what do you get? Try long, lean, supple upper-body muscles that you can show off in sleeveless blouses, backless dresses, and spaghetti straps!

If, like me, you're genetically built like a "pear," with most of your weight settling on your hips and thighs, firming and shaping your upper body will help you to minimize your trouble spots down below. For example, weak, sloping shoulders can make your lower body appear wider. If, however, you firm and fill out your shoulders and upper body, you'll help create a slimmer, trimmer waistline. Your shoulders will taper down to a thin waist and hips.

Upper-body toning creates better body proportions. You'll firm any flab under your arms so it doesn't jiggle when you wave. You'll tone and lift your breasts and create muscle for sexy cleavage. Strengthening your upper back and shoulders helps you to stand upright naturally. The better your posture, the slimmer, taller, and

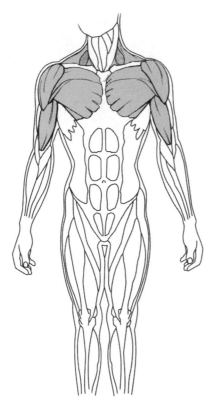

Get bikini-ready biceps—and chest, shoulders, and back—with the ball and band.

more confident you appear. Also, as you firm your upper back, you'll no longer have bra overhang, the fat that pushes out around our bra straps!

Upper-body strength will also help you move through life with more ease. Strong arm, chest, shoulder, and back muscles help you to lift and carry heavy laundry baskets or your growing kids without putting stress on your back.

In this chapter, I'll share my favorite upper-body moves with you. Learning a bit about the anatomy and physiology of your upper body will help you understand why I've designed these exercises in the way I have. You will target the following important upper-body areas.

▶ **Arms.** You'll target your biceps, along the front of your upper arms, and your triceps, along the back of your upper arms.

▶ **Chest.** You'll work your pectoralis major, the muscle that lifts your breasts and gives them definition and shape. Developing your chest helps you create a line of cleavage, because the two sides of your pectoralis muscles meet just above your breasts. Your pectoralis major sits underneath your breast tissue, so it will lift your breasts, helping to counteract the pull of gravity.

▶ **Shoulders.** Working your deltoid muscles along the front, top, and back of your shoulders will help eliminate sloping shoulders, making you look more confident, youthful, and energetic. You'll give yourself natural shoulder pads, creating a strong, sexy look.

▶ **Upper back.** You'll work your trapezius muscle—a large diamond-shaped muscle that begins at the base of your skull, fans out to your shoulders, and extends halfway down your back—and smaller upper-back muscles including the teres minor and infraspinatus. You'll also work your latissimus dorsi (often called lats), which are slightly lower on your back.

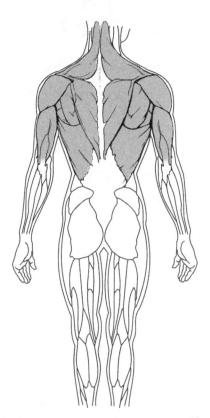

Lift your shoulders by working your deltoids to create a sexy and strong upper back.

I've incorporated the band into all but two exercises. Because of the flexibility of the band, you will find that it challenges your balance just as much as the ball does. Be patient with yourself and perform each exercise slowly. Soon, you will not feel so wobbly.

As you lift and lower the band, try to make smooth, fluid movements rather than quick, jerky ones. Whenever you feel that you need more resistance, you can increase the challenge by grasping the band closer to its middle, which will create more tension and take the exercise to the next level.

Maintain good posture—a long spine, relaxed shoulders, an open chest, and a firm abdomen—in every move.

Perform up to 12 repetitions of each exercise. In a few movements, instead of doing repetitions, you'll simply hold the posture up to 1 minute. When multiple variations of an exercise are shown, try the initial, beginner version first. Some of these exercises are very challenging; don't let that discourage you. In the 3-week plan in part 3, I start you off with beginner exercises during week 1 and gradually build up to intermediate and advanced moves by week 3.

CHEST PRESS

▶ **Tones your chest, back, abdomen, and thighs**

▶ **Lifts your breasts**

In addition to zeroing in on those chest muscles, doing this exercise against the ball gives you a great leg and abdominal workout. You'll really feel the backs of your thighs and buttocks working to keep your hips lifted.

A. Lie with your upper back, neck, and head supported by the ball and with an exercise band secured between your back and the ball. Grasp an end of the band in each hand and wrap it around the hand, with your elbows bent at 90 degrees.

B. Exhale as you press your hands toward the ceiling. Inhale as you lower to the starting position. Continue to press and lower 12 times.

Advanced Chest Press

C. Lifting one leg will challenge your balance, creating a more intense leg and abdomen workout as you press and lower the band. Lift and extend one leg for up to 30 seconds and then switch legs for the remaining 30 seconds.

PUSHUP

► Tones your chest and abdomen

The ball will really challenge you in the pushup. If you can do just a few of these pushups, give yourself a pat on the back!

A. Bring your body into the pushup position with your shins against the ball and your palms on the floor under your chest. (*Note:* Placing your thighs against the ball makes it easier.)

B. Inhale while you lower your chest to the floor by bending your elbows. Stop once your chin is even with the bend in your elbows, then exhale as you press back to the starting position. Keep your back flat, hips up, and abs tight throughout the exercise. Don't allow your hips to sink down or your lower back to arch. Repeat up to 12 times.

Advanced Pushup

C. Lifting one leg will challenge your balance even more. Lift one leg for half of the repetitions, lower it, and then lift the other leg for the remaining repetitions.

{ "The closer you bring the ball
to your thighs, the easier this one is.
Try a few this way first,
and don't give up—you can do it!" }

CHEST FIRMER

▶ **Tones the sides of your chest**

▶ **Firms your back, abdomen, legs, and buttocks**

As with the chest press, the chest firmer gives you a great leg and abdominal workout as the backs of your thighs and buttocks work to keep your hips lifted.

A. Lie with your upper back, neck, and head supported by the ball and with an exercise band secured between your back and the ball. Grasp an end of the band in each hand with your arms extended toward the ceiling. Keep your abs tight.

B. Inhale as you lower your arms out to the sides. Exhale as you press your hands back together above your chest, as if you were squeezing a large beach ball around your chest. Continue to lower and raise your hands 12 times.

UPPER-BACK FIRMER

▶ **Tones your upper back**

▶ **Strengthens your legs**

▶ **Stretches your hips and thighs**

You'll tone your upper and lower body at once by doing a lunge over the ball as you simultaneously "unsheathe your sword."

A. Stand with your feet under your hips. Step forward about 2 to 3 feet with your right leg. Place the ball under your right thigh. Exhale as you bend your right leg and sink into a deep lunge. Inhale and lift your left heel and move it inward, so that your rear foot is at a 45-degree angle. Grasp one end of the band in your left hand, resting your hand along your outer left thigh. Grasp the other end of the band in your right hand and position that hand near your left hipbone.

B. Exhale as you unsheathe your imaginary sword and raise it overhead. Inhale as you release. Repeat six times and then switch sides.

ARM ROW

Firms and shapes your upper back

I call this my "no more bra-overhang" exercise. It targets the piece of flab that tends to bunch outward from your bra strap.

A. From a standing position, secure the band under your left foot, grasping both ends in your right hand. Place your left palm on top of the ball and your left leg next to the ball. Take a large step back with your right leg and bend forward about 45 degrees. Extend your right arm toward the floor. Tighten your abs.

B. Exhale as you raise your right elbow toward the ceiling, as if you were starting a lawn mower. Inhale as you lower it. Repeat 12 times and then switch sides.

Intermediate Arm Row

C. Doing the same exercise with your rear foot on the ball really challenges your balance. You'll feel muscles up and down your torso firming to help keep you upright. You'll also strengthen your standing leg.

To get into position, stand and secure the band under your right foot. Grasp an end of the band in each hand. Bend your left knee and place the top of your left foot against the ball. Roll the ball behind your torso as you extend your left leg behind. Bend forward about 45 degrees, as shown. Exhale as you raise your elbows toward the ceiling, as if you were rowing a boat. Inhale as you lower.

Advanced Arm Row

D. Doing this same exercise while in an arabesque position but without the ball will improve your balance and firm just about every muscle in your body. To get into position, secure the middle of the band under your left foot, grasping an end of the band in each hand. Step back with your right foot so that your feet are about 2 feet apart. Shift your body weight over your left foot. Slowly lift your right foot off the floor as you bend your torso forward, coming into the arabesque position. Try to keep your hips level, not allowing your left hipbone to rise up. Raise your elbows toward the ceiling as you exhale, and lower as you inhale.

LATERAL RAISE

► Tones and strengthens your shoulders

Sitting on the ball will work your abdomen as you raise and lower the band, shaping beautiful, sexy shoulders.

A. Sit on the ball with your back straight, abs tight, and an exercise band secured between your feet and the ground. Grasp an end of the band in each hand, with your arms fully extended by your hips and your palms facing the ball.

B. Exhale as you raise your arms out to your sides, with your palms facing down, until they are level with your shoulders. Inhale as you lower to the starting position. Continue to raise and lower 12 times.

Intermediate Lateral Raise

C. Lifting and extending one leg will put you off balance, forcing your tummy, waist, and back to work to keep you upright. You will also strengthen the fronts of your thighs. Secure the band under one foot, raising and extending the opposite leg. Raise and lower the band six times. Then switch legs and complete six more repetitions.

FRONT RAISE

► **Tones and strengthens your shoulders**

The front raise will help you sculpt the fronts of your shoulders as you simultaneously target your abdomen.

A. Sit on the ball with your back straight and an exercise band secured under your feet. Grasp an end of the band in each hand, with your arms fully extended by your hips and your palms facing the ball. Tighten your abs.

B. Exhale as you raise your arms straight out in front of you, with your thumbs pointing up, until they are level with your shoulders. Inhale as you lower to the starting position. Continue to raise and lower 12 times.

Intermediate Front Raise

C. Lifting and extending one leg will put you off balance, forcing your tummy, waist, and back to work to keep you upright. You'll also strengthen the fronts of your thighs. Secure the band under one foot, raising and extending the opposite leg. Raise and lower the band six times. Then switch legs and complete six more repetitions.

{ "Work your belly, thighs, and shoulders—all at once." }

UPPER-BACK TONER

► **Strengthens and tones your upper back and upper arms**

As with previous seated exercises, the ball will work your core muscles as you raise and lower the band.

A. Sit on the ball and bend forward about 45 degrees. Secure the resistance band under your feet. Cross the band so that you are grasping the band's left end in your right hand and the band's right end in your left hand. Extend your arms toward the floor with your palms facing in.

B. Exhale as you raise your arms up and out to the sides until they are level with your shoulders. Inhale as you lower to the starting position. Continue to raise and lower 12 times.

BACK AND SHOULDER FIRMER

Strengthens and tones your upper back and shoulders

This is a great exercise that helps to really shape the shoulders. As you raise your arms overhead, you'll feel your torso firm as it works to stabilize you on the ball.

A. Cross the band so that you are grasping the band's left end in your right hand and the band's right end in your left hand. Extend your arms toward the floor with your knuckles facing forward.

B. Exhale as you raise your arms out to the sides and up overhead, keeping your thumbs up the entire time. Keep your shoulders relaxed away from your ears and your spine long. Inhale as you lower to the starting position. Repeat 12 times.

UPRIGHT ROW

▶ **Firms your upper back and shoulders**

Sculpt a beautiful line along the tops of your shoulders with this exercise as you simultaneously firm up your abdomen.

A. Sit on the ball with your back straight and the exercise band secured under your feet. Grasp an end of the band in each hand, with your arms fully extended and hands near your knees.

B. Exhale as you raise your elbows toward the ceiling and your hands toward your chin. Keep your back straight and shoulders relaxed away from your ears. Inhale as you lower to the starting position. Repeat 12 times.

Intermediate Upright Row

C. Doing upright rows in an inclined position forces your core muscles to work harder to keep you balanced. You'll also strengthen your legs. Sit on the ball with your knees bent and feet on the floor. Walk your feet forward as you slide down the ball, until your lower back rests against the ball. Your feet should be far enough away from the ball for your thighs to be parallel with the floor. Then secure the band under your feet to perform the upright rows, as shown.

OVERHEAD PRESS

► Firms and shapes your shoulders

This will give you a beautiful figure, a strong and sexy upper body. As with previous seated exercises, the ball will work your core muscles as you raise and lower the band.

A. Sit on the ball. Secure the middle of the resistance band under your feet. Grasp the ends of the band with your elbows bent and hands in front of your shoulders, palms facing forward.

B. Exhale as you raise your hands above your head. Keep your shoulders relaxed away from your ears as you do so. Inhale as you lower to the starting position. Repeat 12 times.

Intermediate Overhead Press

C. Lifting and extending one leg will put you off balance, forcing your tummy, waist, and back to work to keep you upright. You'll also strengthen the fronts of your thighs. Secure the band under one foot, raising and extending the opposite leg. Raise and lower the band six times. Then switch legs and complete six more repetitions.

Advanced Overhead Press

D. Lowering one arm at a time forces your shoulders to work twice as hard. Sit on the ball. Secure the middle of the resistance band under both feet. Grasp the ends of the band with your elbows bent and hands just in front of your shoulders, palms facing forward. Exhale as you raise your hands above your head. Keep your right arm extended as you inhale and lower the left. Exhale as you raise your left hand and then inhale as you lower the right. Keep one arm extended overhead at all times. Do 12 total repetitions.

TRICEPS KICKBACK

► **Firms the backs of your upper arms**

► **Tones your torso**

Keep your abs toned and lifted while you firm up the backs of your arms.

A. Sit on the ball and bend forward about 45 degrees. Secure the resistance band under your feet. Grasp the ends of the band in your hands with your arms extended toward the floor and palms facing in. Bring your elbows up toward the ceiling and your hands in toward your ribs, as shown.

B. Exhale as you extend your arms behind your torso. Inhale as you return to the starting position. Try to keep your upper arms and shoulders motionless, bending only at the elbows. Repeat 12 times.

ARM FIRMER

Tones the backs of your upper arms and shoulders

▸

No more underarm flab; no more underarm sag. This exercise will firm up your arms.

A. Sit on the ball with your knees bent and feet on the floor. Grasp the middle of the band in your left hand, holding your hand by your left hip. Grasp one end of the band in your right hand. Extend your right arm from your chest with your palm facing down, as shown. If this feels too challenging, you can release some of the band with your left hand to provide less resistance.

B. Inhale as you bend your right elbow and bring your right hand toward your left shoulder. Exhale as you extend your right arm back to the starting position. Repeat six times and then switch sides.

FRENCH CURL

▶ **Tones the backs of your upper arms**

▶ **Firms your core muscles**

This French curl and all of the variations are great ways to firm up your arms. Doing it overhead like this makes it target the length of your triceps.

A. Sit on the ball with the middle of the resistance band secured under your feet. Grasp an end of the band in each hand. Extend your arms overhead, palms facing each other. Keep your abs engaged.

B. Inhale as you bend your elbows and lower your hands behind your head. Exhale as you raise your hands back to the starting position. Repeat 12 times.

Intermediate French Curl

C. When you alternate arms, you make them work twice as hard. To get into position, sit on the ball with the middle of the resistance band secured under your feet. Grasp an end of the band in each hand. Extend your arms overhead. Inhale as you bend one elbow and lower that hand behind your head, as shown. Exhale as you extend that arm back up and then lower the other, alternating arms for 12 repetitions.

Advanced French Curl

D. You can also do French curls without the ball. Doing them while standing stretches the band a bit more, making it tighter and creating more resistance to the exercise. To get into position, stand in a lunge position with your left foot forward. Secure the middle of the band under your right foot. Grasp an end of the band in each hand. Extend your arms overhead. Inhale as you bend your elbows and lower your hands behind your head, as shown. Exhale as you extend them overhead.

BICEPS CURL

▶ **Firms the fronts of your upper arms**

Doing biceps curls with a resistance band gives you a better workout, because there's both a positive and a negative resistance. A dumbbell lets gravity pull it down, but the band uses more muscles to both raise *and* lower.

A. Sit on the ball with the resistance band secured under your feet. Grasp an end of the band in each hand, with your arms fully extended toward the floor and your palms facing away from your torso.

B. Exhale as you bend your arms and lift your hands to your shoulders. Inhale as you lower to the starting position. Repeat 12 times.

Intermediate Biceps Curl

C. Lifting and extending one leg will take you off balance, making your core muscles work harder to keep you steady. Do six repetitions with one leg extended and then switch legs for six more reps.

HAMMER CURL

▶ **Firms the fronts of your upper arms**

▶ **Gives you beautiful, sexy arms**

Hammer curls target a slightly different section of the biceps muscle. Doing both traditional curls and hammer curls will help to truly shape your biceps.

A. Sit on the ball with the resistance band secured under your feet. Grasp an end of the band in each hand, with your arms fully extended toward the floor, your palms facing the ball, and your thumbs up. Keep your abs tight.

B. Exhale as you bend your arms and lift your hands to your shoulders. Inhale as you lower to the starting position. Repeat 12 times.

LAT PULLDOWN

▶ **Tones your chest and back**

▶ **Strengthens your lats**

Holding the ball will help you to extend more fully into the lat pulldown as well as to keep your shoulders in position, making the exercise more effective.

A. Lie on your back with your knees bent and feet on the floor. Grasp the ball and extend your arms and the ball above your chest.

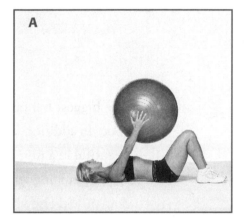

B. Inhale as you lower the ball behind your head. Exhale as you raise it. Keep your hips steady and lower back against the floor the entire time. Repeat 12 times.

STRETCHING ON THE BALL

Elongate and soothe your muscles

The biggest benefit of stretching is how it makes you feel: oh so good. In addition, a regular stretching routine can make you more beautiful in a number of ways. First, it helps to improve your posture. Stretching lengthens the muscles in your legs, hips, back, abdomen, and elsewhere, helping you to stand taller. As your muscles lengthen, you'll feel less pain and stiffness. You will move more fluidly and be able to enjoy other kinds of fitness activities. Stretching also increases blood circulation throughout your body. Good circulation helps heal your body and reduces swelling. Stretching is also a perfect way to eliminate tension in your muscles. After sitting all day at the office, a short stretching routine can help put a spring back in your step. Any time you need a natural energy boost, just take a stretch break.

The following routine stretches all of the major muscles in your body, specifically:

▸ **Your chest and shoulders.** Tight chest muscles can cause us to slouch and collapse our shoulders forward. This, in turn, restricts breathing, which causes fatigue. These chest and shoulder stretches will help you to sit and stand upright with better posture, giving yourself a burst of energy.

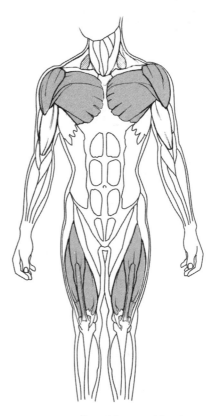

Counter stress, slouching, and back pain with stretches aimed at your chest, shoulders, and thighs.

▸ **Your upper back.** Have you ever felt sore or tight between your shoulder blades? I often do. The stretches in the beginning of the routine—the hug-a-ball and the upper-back stretch—are among my favorite stability-ball stretches because they target this area of the back so well. They warm up your trapezius and rhomboid muscles in your upper back and help work the kinks out of your shoulder blades. You will love them.

▸ **Your lower back and spine.** For optimal health of the disks in your spine, you must move your back in four directions: forward, backward, to the side, and in rotation. I made sure these stretches will move your spine through its fullest range of motion, helping you to keep your spine and back healthy.

▸ **Your thighs.** Tight muscles in the fronts, sides, or backs of the thighs tend to tug the pelvis out of alignment, creating back pain. This routine will help you stretch and lengthen your thighs, taking tension off your back and helping to sculpt longer, leaner legs.

▸ **Your hips.** We tend to hold a lot of tension in our hips, and many fitness pursuits such as running tend to make them even tighter. I've incorporated

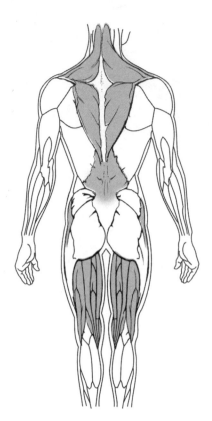

Feel your body release tension all over as you welcome invigorating blood flow back into all your muscles.

two of my favorite hip stretches—the hip stretch and the hip release—into this routine to help release tension from those areas. They feel wonderful!

This routine is a collection of my favorite stretches that I turn to day in and out to elongate my muscles and feel good all over. Do this routine in the morning to wake up your body, before or after a cardio workout, or before or after your toning workout.

You can either flow through this sequence a few times, holding each position for a few seconds, or hold each stretch for a longer period of time—20 to 30 seconds. In this series of movements, the ball and band will serve as props that help you more easily stretch into certain positions, ones that would be more challenging without these two tools. In some stretches, the ball helps you move your body into proper alignment, so you can make the most of each stretch. Finally, adding the band in some of the stretches helps you warm up and stretch particular muscles through their entire range of motion, instead of only in one direction.

Move into each stretch slowly, paying close attention to your own internal cues. Try to challenge your muscles enough to lengthen them, but don't overchallenge them.

As you stretch, breathe deeply and smoothly, never holding your breath. Don't bounce or jerk your body into a stretch. Just slowly bring your body into the stretch, surrender to it, and let your muscles respond gradually. Be gentle and enjoy the feeling of your body lengthening and rejuvenating!

HUG-A-BALL

▶ **Stretches your upper back and shoulders**

▶ **Elongates the spine and opens the back, giving space to each vertebra**

This stretch is so simple, yet it feels so wonderful.

A. Stand while holding the stability ball against your navel. Rest your arms over the top of the ball and use your palms to press the ball to your tummy. Inhale as you lengthen your spine upward. Pull in your navel and engage your abs.

B. Exhale as you bend your knees slightly, curl your chin toward your chest, and fold your torso against the ball. Spread your shoulder blades apart and round your spine. Hold up to 30 seconds, breathing normally.

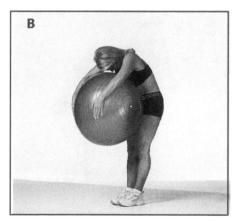

UPPER-BACK STRETCH

▶ **Stretches your upper back and shoulders**

▶ **Releases tension between your shoulder blades**

Holding the ball in front of your body will help keep your arms in the right position.

A. Stand with your feet under your hips and your arms and ball extended at chest level.

B. Exhale as you bring your navel toward your spine and curl forward, keeping your arms by your ears as you do so. Inhale as you rise. Repeat curling and rising for 1 minute.

WAIST ROTATION/LOWER-BACK STRETCH

► **Stretches your lower back**

► **Conditions your spine**

Holding the ball in front of your body as you twist will help you to keep your spine long and your chest open.

A. Stand with your feet under your hips. Grasp the ball between your hands, extending both arms out from your chest. Inhale as you firm your tummy and lengthen your spine. Exhale as you rotate your torso to the left, starting at the base of your spine and moving upward, as shown. Inhale as you return to center.

B. Exhale as you rotate to the right, as shown. Continue rotating from one side to the other for 1 minute.

SIDE STRETCH

▶ **Stretches your sides**

▶ **Strengthens your tummy**

Holding the ball overhead will help you to keep your shoulders in the proper position as you stretch. This stretch is great for lengthening your spine.

A. Stand with your feet under your hips and your arms and ball extended overhead. Relax your shoulders away from your ears. Inhale as you firm your tummy and lengthen your spine.

B. Exhale as you bend to the left, as shown, keeping your chest open and your right shoulder blade stacked above the left. Maintain equal weight in both feet. Turn your head to look up. Inhale as you rise to the starting position and then exhale as you bend to the right. Continue bending left and right for 1 minute.

THIGH STRETCH

Lengthens the backs of your thighs

This half-forward bend allows you to safely and slowly stretch the backs of your thighs without stressing your lower back.

A. Stand with your feet under your hips and with the ball 1 or 2 feet in front of you. Bend forward from the hips and place both palms on top of the ball. Exhale as you bend forward even more, moving the ball forward along the floor. Hold for 20 to 30 seconds, breathing normally. Inhale as you rise.

{ "This is one stretch I <u>really</u> love." }

SPINE STRETCH

► **Stretches your chest and shoulders**

► **Lengthens your spine**

This variation of yoga's child's pose encourages you to extend back through your tailbone, feeling the nice, long stretch through each vertebra in your spine.

A. Kneel on your shins and place both palms on the ball. Exhale as you extend your arms and bend forward, rolling the ball forward, until your torso is nearly parallel to the floor.

Once in position, extend back through your tailbone and forward through the top of your head and fingertips. Allow your shoulder blades to widen away from each other and your chest to open. Hold for 20 to 30 seconds, breathing normally. Inhale as you rise.

SPINAL TWIST

▶ **Stretches your sides and waist**

▶ **Conditions your spine**

You would normally do the spinal twist with your hands against the floor. Doing it on the ball allows you to focus specifically on rotating your spine, deepening the stretch.

A. Stand with your legs under your hips. Place both palms on the ball and roll the ball forward as you bend forward from the hips.

Keep your right palm against the ball as you exhale and raise your left arm toward the ceiling, as shown, opening your chest and twisting your spine. Keep equal weight on both feet. Hold for 30 seconds, breathing normally. Inhale as you return to the starting position. Then exhale as you lift your right arm toward the ceiling.

TORSO STRETCH

► **Stretches your chest, shoulders, sides, back, and legs**

The ball's roundness allows you to easily roll it from one side to another, bringing your body into some positions that you could never do without the support of the ball. This stretch is a great example. You'll stretch muscles in your back that have become tight from sitting all day long. It feels wonderful.

A. Stand with your legs under your hips. Place the ball in front of you. Bend forward from your hips and place your palms against the ball. Roll the ball in a semicircle toward your right foot, as shown. As the ball rolls, your left hand will rise and right hand lower. Hold for 20 to 30 seconds, breathing normally.

B. Roll the ball in a semicircle to your left foot and hold for 20 to 30 seconds.

FRONT-OF-THIGH STRETCH

▶ **Stretches the fronts of your thighs**

▶ **Strengthens your hips and thighs**

The ball helps to steady your balance in this traditional thigh stretch.

A. Stand with your feet under your hips and the ball to your right side. Place your right palm or fingertips against the ball. Inhale as you bend your left knee and lift your left foot toward your buttocks. Exhale as you grasp your left foot with your left hand, as shown, and gently pull it closer to your hips. Hold for 20 to 30 seconds and then release and repeat on the other side.

HIP RELEASE

► **Warms up your lower back and hips**

Only the ball allows you to roll your hips in these soothing, gentle circles. I love doing this hip release first thing in the morning or whenever my hips begin to feel tight.

A. Sit on the ball with your knees bent and feet on the floor. Extend your arms out to the sides at shoulder height, as shown. Exhale as you tuck your tailbone and begin to circle your hips in a clockwise motion.

B. Continue to circle your hips all the way around, exhaling as you tuck your tailbone and inhaling as you release the tuck. Do this for 20 to 30 seconds. Then reverse direction for 20 to 30 seconds.

HIP STRETCH

▶ Stretches your hips and buttocks

This is one of my favorite stretches. It targets a deep muscle in your buttocks that is often responsible for causing back and sciatic discomfort.

A. Sit on the ball with your knees bent and feet on the floor. Bend and lift your right leg, placing your right ankle just above your left knee, as shown. Turn out your right knee.

B. Slide down the ball until the ball comes in contact with your lower back, as shown. Make sure your knee is bent at a 90-degree angle. Place one or both hands on the floor for support. Hold for 20 to 30 seconds, rise, and repeat on the opposite leg.

HAMSTRING STRETCH

▶ **Stretches the backs of your thighs**

This stretch is similar to one that you can do while seated on the floor. I find, however, that it feels much better while seated on the ball. Try it both ways, and I'm sure you'll agree.

A. Sit on the ball with your legs spread apart in a wide angle, forming a V shape, and your toes pointing up. Exhale as you bend forward from the hips and slide your hands down your legs until your fingers reach the floor. Try to keep your back long and flat. Hold for 20 to 30 seconds, breathing normally.

B. Keeping your back long and flat, exhale as you walk your hands over to your left foot. Shift your torso and bend your belly over your left thigh. Hold for 20 to 30 seconds, breathing normally.

C. Exhale as you walk your hands over to your right foot. Hold for 20 to 30 seconds. Return to the center position and then inhale as you rise.

{ "I love this stretch so much, I do it almost every day." }

SHOULDER STRETCH

► **Stretches your chest and shoulders**

The band allows you to stretch your shoulders through a wider range of motion than you probably ever thought possible. Because the band stretches with you, it allows you to slowly and gently move your hands farther apart as you bring your arms in a semicircle.

A. Sit on the ball with your knees bent and feet on the floor. Hold the ends of the band in each hand and gather up the material until the band feels taut.

B. Inhale as you raise your arms up overhead.

C. Exhale as you lower the band behind your torso, as shown. Inhale as you raise your arms back overhead, and exhale as you return to the starting position. Continue to alternate between the two positions for 20 to 30 seconds.

{ *"Give your shoulders the break they—and you—deserve!"* }

CHEST STRETCH

▶ **Stretches your chest**

▶ **Strengthens your upper arms**

You can also do this stretch while standing, but I find it feels much more comfortable when seated on the ball.

A. Sit on the ball with your knees bent and feet on the floor. Clasp your hands behind your back. Inhale as you roll your shoulders up, back, and then down. Reach down through your knuckles, squeeze your shoulder blades together, and lift your sternum.

B. Exhale as you bend forward, bringing your tummy onto your thighs. Lift your arms as you reach through your knuckles to increase the stretch. Hold for 20 to 30 seconds, breathing normally. Inhale as you rise.

ARM STRETCH

► **Stretches the tops of your arms and shoulders**

► **Gives you great flexibility in your triceps**

The band serves as a great tool in this stretch. Without the band, you'd need the flexibility to be able to grasp your hands behind your back!

A. Sit on the ball with your knees bent and feet on the floor. Grasp the band in your right hand.

Raise your right arm overhead, bringing the top of your right arm near your right ear. Bend your right elbow and bring your right palm toward your shoulder blade, as if you were giving yourself a pat on the back. Bring your left arm and hand behind your back from below and grasp the band. Hold for 20 to 30 seconds, breathing normally. Slowly take up more and more of the band as you inch your hands toward one another and deepen the stretch. Keep your shoulders relaxed away from your ears and your spine long. Switch arm positions and repeat.

CHILD'S POSE

▶ **Stretches your hips, back, spine, chest, and shoulders**

The ball will encourage you to reach forward, allowing you to feel a deeper stretch in your upper back and shoulders. It also allows you to open your chest to one side, creating a wonderful stretch along the side of your torso. Once you do this with the ball, you may never go back to the floor!

A. Kneel with your hips on top of your heels and shins against the floor. Place both palms on the top of the ball. Reach forward, extending your arms and rolling the ball as far forward as you can without lifting your hips off your heels.

B. Exhale as you lower your right hand and raise your left, rotating your torso to the right. Hold for 30 seconds. Inhale as you return to the starting position and then exhale as you rotate to the left. Hold for 30 seconds.

PILATES ON THE BALL

Sculpt, stretch, and elongate your muscles

Named after Joseph Pilates, who invented the method more than 80 years ago, Pilates involves a series of exercises that place intense concentration on your abdominal muscles, particularly the deepest layer of muscle in your abdomen. I love Pilates because it strengthens and stretches my body from head to toe and helps me to emphasize the core muscles in my abdomen, waistline, and back. It also helps me to maintain my rock-hard tummy.

When you add the ball and band to traditional Pilates movements, you gain all of those benefits and more. Specifically, the ball and band will help you to stretch and sculpt the following body areas.

▸ **Your abdomen and back.** As you perform traditional Pilates movements with your abdomen, backsides, hips, or legs against the ball, your core muscles must work even harder to keep your body stable. As you balance your body weight, you'll zero in on your transverse abdominis, a deep abdominal muscle that is hard to target with other toning

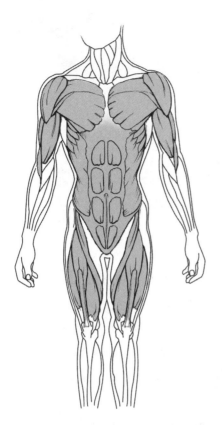

Pilates is truly a total-body workout, targeting muscles throughout your body, all at once.

exercises. Your transverse abdominis acts like a corset to hold your abdominal organs in place. The stronger this muscle is, the smaller your waistline and the flatter your tummy!

▸ **Your arms and shoulders.** Adding the band helps to tone your upper body. Two moves in particular—the bug (page 139) and the rowing series (page 150)—will strengthen your arms, shoulders, and upper back. Another movement, the plank (page 143), will target your arms and chest.

▸ **Your legs.** I've included the Pilates leg series in this routine. It will help to slim your thighs and tone away saddlebags. It particularly zeros in on the abductor muscles along your outer thighs and the adductor muscles along your inner thighs. You'll sculpt lean, toned, beautiful legs in just a few movements.

In addition to making some Pilates movements more effective (and a bit more challenging), the ball and band will also help to make some Pilates movements more accessible. In these exercises, such as the T-stand (page 140), the ball serves as an aid that helps you train your body to be able to hold the traditional posture.

The best part of all is that the band will help you to align your body correctly, giving you the feedback you need to extend more fully into the posture. I love using the band when I do Pilates because it's a safe and gentle source of resistance. The band serves as the perfect complement, allowing you to create smooth, circular, flowing movements. You'll feel as if you were dancing.

In the following pages, you'll find 13 of my favorite Pilates moves. All of them include the ball, and some incorporate the band. You can do all 13 movements in sequence to stretch and tone your legs, back, abdomen, waistline, shoulders, upper back, arms, and shoulders. These moves will also show up in the 3-week plan, or you can pick and choose the moves you like the most to incorporate into a workout you design yourself (chapter 9 will show you how).

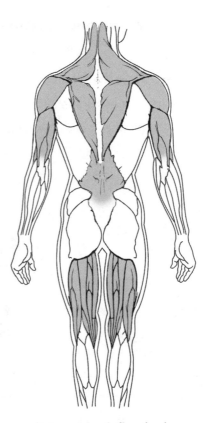

See results in your waistline, back, arms, neck, and lower-body toning by using these Pilates-based exercises.

{ "Feel your navel pull in, your abs contract, and keep a neutral spine . . ." }

PILATES TUMMY TUCK

You'll love the sensation of this stretch. The support of the ball allows you to create a full arch in your spine, stretching out that area between the shoulder blades that can become so tight after a day of working at a computer.

A. Stand with your feet together. Bend forward from the hips and place your palms on top of the stability ball. Inhale as you roll the ball forward and lengthen your spine, stretching your head and tailbone away from each other.

B. Exhale as you curl your chin and tailbone toward each other, firming your abs, keeping your navel in, and arching your spine upward. At the same time, bring the ball back in toward your legs. Continue to alternate between the two positions for 1 minute.

PILATES TWIST

▶ **Tones your waistline**

▶ **Stretches your spine, back, and chest**

The ball will keep you a little off balance during the Pilates twist, forcing more muscle fibers in your abdomen to work to keep you stable. The band will keep your arms and shoulders aligned properly.

A. Sit on your ball with your knees bent and feet on the floor. Grasp an end of the band in each hand and extend your arms out to your sides at shoulder level with the band behind your upper back. Firm your abs, inhale, and lengthen your spine, reaching your head upward as you grow taller.

B. Exhale as you twist to the left, feeling the twist start at the base of your spine and move upward, as if your spine were a spiral staircase. Inhale as you return to the starting position and then exhale as you twist to the other side. Continue to alternate sides for 1 minute.

SAW

▶ **Slims your waistline and strengthens your abdomen**

▶ **Stretches your back and chest**

Using the ball during the saw takes the movement to a new level. You'll really feel your waistline working to keep your torso stable as you twist. The band will help hold your arms in the proper position, preventing your top shoulder from rolling inward.

A. Sit on the ball with your legs extended in a wide angle. Grasp an end of the band in each hand and extend your arms out to your sides, with the band behind your upper back. Inhale and lengthen your spine, reaching your head upward as you grow taller. Pull in your navel and engage your abs.

B. Exhale as you twist your torso, "sawing" your right pinkie finger past your left pinkie toe. Inhale as you rise to the starting position. Exhale as you repeat on the other side. Keep your abdominal muscles active and your spine extended throughout the movement. Alternate sides for 1 minute.

BUG

Tones your shoulders, arms, and upper back

The resistance of the band helps tone your shoulders as you smoothly swing your arms forward and back. The ball will challenge your balance, targeting your abs. The ball allows you to flatten your tummy as you firm and strengthen your upper body.

A. Sit on the ball with your knees bent and feet on the floor. Place the middle of the band under your feet. Grasp one end of the band in each hand. Bend forward from the hips about 45 degrees. Keep abs active.

Exhale as you raise your right arm forward and your left arm back, as shown, until both arms are parallel to the floor. Inhale as you switch positions, bringing your right arm back and left arm forward. Continue to alternate positions for 1 minute.

T-STAND

▶ **Trims your waistline**

▶ **Improves your balance and coordination**

Many people struggle to hold a full T-stand for even just a few seconds. Doing it with the ball, however, allows you to extend into the T-stand and hold it much longer.

A. Lie with your left side on the ball and your legs extended, one on top of the other. Exhale as you press your left palm into the floor and extend your right arm toward the ceiling. Turn your head to look up toward the ceiling. Try to lift the side of your torso so that the ball merely provides feedback and some help with balance. Don't allow your torso to collapse against the ball. Hold for 30 seconds, breathing normally, and then switch sides.

FRONT/BACK

Tones your outer thighs, waistline, and abdomen

Doing the front/back against the ball challenges your torso to keep your body steady as you move your leg forward and back.

A. Lie with your left side on the ball and your left knee on the floor. Press your left hand into the floor. Lift and extend your right leg until it is even with your torso. Rest your right palm against the ball. Exhale as you bring your right leg forward, as shown, keeping your abdomen firm and your torso steady.

B. Inhale as you bring your right leg back behind the ball. Try to keep your torso and hips motionless as you move your leg. Continue to bring it front and back for 30 seconds and then switch sides.

HIP CIRCLES

► **Tone your outer thighs, waistline, and abdomen**

As with the front/back, doing hip circles against the ball challenges your torso to keep your body steady as you move your leg.

A. Lie with your left side on the ball and your left knee on the floor. Press your left hand into the floor. Lift and extend your right leg until it is even with your torso, as shown.

Circle your right leg slowly, with control, exhaling as your leg comes forward and inhaling as it circles back and up. Keep your abdomen firm and your torso steady as you do so. Continue to circle your leg for 30 seconds and then switch sides.

PILATES PLANK

▶ **Tones your upper body, abdomen, and legs**

▶ **Targets the hard-to-firm transverse abdominis**

Placing your feet on the ball adds quite a challenge to the traditional plank. If you've never felt your abdomen work to hold you up during a traditional plank, you'll definitely feel those muscles fire with your feet on the ball.

A. Come into a pushup position with your thighs, shins, or feet against the ball and your palms on the floor under your chest. (The farther down on your legs you position the ball, the more challenging the exercise.) Hold for 1 minute, breathing normally. Keep your navel in, abdomen firm, and back flat and extended. Try not to let your hips sink down or rise above the plane between your feet and head.

Intermediate Pilates Plank

B. Lifting one leg increases the challenge to your balance and tones your thighs and buttocks. Come into the plank position with your thighs, shins, or feet against the ball and your palms on the floor under your chest. Exhale as you lift one leg. Hold for 30 seconds (or as long as you can) and then switch legs.

ROLL-DOWN

▶ **Tones your abdomen**

▶ **Conditions your spine**

▶ **Stretches your legs and back**

Doing the roll-down with the ball overhead prevents you from cheating. You'll really feel your tummy working when you do this exercise!

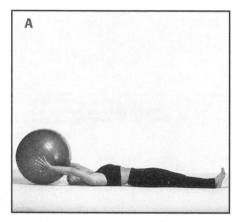

A. Lie on your back with your legs extended. Grasp the ball with your palms and hold it behind your head. Inhale as you firm your abdomen and lengthen your spine.

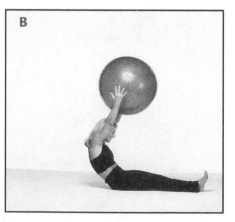

B. Inhale as you tuck your tailbone, bring your navel in toward your spine, and slowly roll up, keeping the ball overhead.

C. Come to a seated position with the ball still overhead and both legs extended. Pull your navel in and keep your abs engaged.

D. Exhale as you stretch forward, bringing the ball to and beyond your feet. Then roll back down. Continue to roll up and then back down for 1 minute.

TEASER

Tones your back, abdomen, and legs

Holding the ball overhead during the teaser helps you to tease your strength and balance a little more. It also helps you extend your torso and arms in the up position, increasing the benefits of the posture.

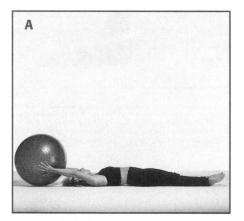

A. Lie on your back with your legs extended. Extend your arms behind your head with the ball between your palms.

B. Exhale as you lift your legs and arms, bringing your body into a V shape. Hold for 5 to 15 seconds. Try to keep your torso long, your abs firm, and your back flat. Release and repeat three or four times.

LEG CIRCLES WITH BALL

▶ **Tone and stretch your legs**

▶ **Strengthen your abdomen**

Adding the ball and band to the leg circles provides many benefits. Placing one leg on the ball helps you keep your hips steady as you circle your other leg. The ball will also move around under your leg, challenging your balance and stability. The band will provide additional resistance as well as some feedback, helping you to feel whether you are making smooth or jerky circles.

A. Lie on your back. Place your left heel on the ball. Wrap the middle of the resistance band around the arch of your right foot. Hold the ends of the band in your right hand. Place both hands out to your sides at a 45-degree angle to your lower torso. Extend your right leg toward the ceiling.

B. Slowly bring your right leg through large clockwise circles, exhaling as you lower your leg (move it from the 12 o'clock to 6 o'clock position) and inhaling as you raise it (move from 6 o'clock to 12 o'clock). Draw six circles in this direction. Then draw six counterclockwise circles. Switch legs and repeat on the other side.

DOUBLE-LEG STRETCH

▶ **Tones your upper and lower tummy**

The ball will encourage you to extend through your arms and legs as you move in and out of this stretch. It also makes the exercise feel smooth and almost meditative as you hand off the ball from your hands to your feet.

A. Lie on your back with your legs extended and raised, as shown. Extend your arms overhead with the ball between your palms.

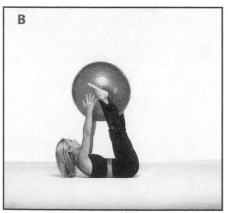

B. Inhale as you lift the ball toward your torso, simultaneously lifting your legs to meet it. Keep your abs engaged and navel in.

C. Exchange the ball from your hands to between your shins. Then exhale as you slowly lower the ball and your legs to the floor, as shown, and extend your arms behind your head. Tap the ball against the floor and then raise your legs and arms back up to pass the ball back to your hands. Continue to exchange the ball from your hands to your feet and from your feet to your hands for 1 minute.

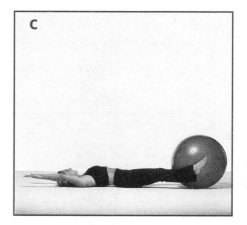

{ *"This is a fabulous exercise."* }

ROWING SERIES

Tones your arms, shoulders, and back

I love the fluid feeling this exercise creates as I circle my arms through the motion. It feels very peaceful as I flow through the sequence. Plus, it tones everything up!

A. Sit on the ball. Bend over at the waist as far as you can (while maintaining a straight back). Secure the exercise band under your feet. Grasp one end of the band in each hand while bent over. Exhale as you raise your body into a sitting position and pull your hands straight up under your chin, as shown, bringing your elbows out to the sides.

B. Inhale as you bend forward again and simultaneously extend your hands behind you. Pull your navel in and tighten your abs.

C. Keeping your arms straight and level with your shoulders, exhale as you move them forward in a half-circle around your body.

D. Keep moving them forward until they are directly in front of your shoulders, as shown. Inhale as you lower to the starting position. Continue to flow through the sequence for 1 minute.

YOGA ON THE BALL

Strengthen and stretch your entire body

▼

Everyone I speak with feels fantastic after doing yoga. This great form of exercise stretches and strengthens your muscles simultaneously. Adding in the ball and band allows beginners and advanced students alike to explore yoga postures in a new way. In the following pages, I've incorporated the ball and band into my favorite yoga postures such as the warrior (pages 156 and 158), the balancing stick (page 162), the mermaid (page 163), and more.

The exercises run in a flow sequence, and you can do the entire sequence as a 12-minute routine, holding each move for up to 1 minute. You can also deepen and hold each pose longer for added benefits—a great alternative when you have more than 12 minutes for your routine.

As with many other exercises that you've learned so far, the ball will keep you slightly off balance and help you work myriad muscles throughout your body, muscles that you wouldn't be able to target if you were doing the same yoga posture without the ball. This is yet another reason that the ball and band are so great. As promised, they really allow you to do quick and very effective workouts.

In particular, this routine will help you zero in on the following areas.

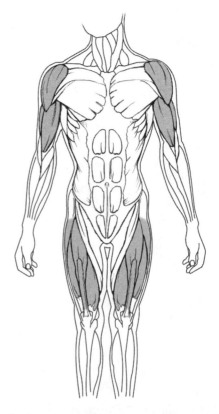

Sculpt long and strong biceps, triceps, and deltoid muscles (as well as lean and defined thighs) with the strengthening and stretching action of yoga.

▶ **Your shoulders and arms.** In numerous exercises, such as the warrior and the triangle, you'll hold your arms out to the sides as you resist the effects of gravity. This will help to sculpt beautiful and sexy arm muscles. You'll strengthen your arms further whenever you lean one or both hands into the ball, such as with the pose of the dancer and the balancing stick.

▶ **Your thighs and buns.** Yoga postures such as the triangle, the warrior, and the balancing stick are well-known for their ability to sculpt what has come to be known as yoga buns. The ball will help you extend into these challenging standing postures, offering support where you need it most and helping to steady your body. You'll be able to focus your mind on extending, lengthening, and releasing into the posture and on holding for longer periods of time.

▶ **Your back and spine.** I've incorporated into this routine stretching and strengthening postures that will move your spine through its entire range of motion. The support of the ball allows you to perform gentle back bends

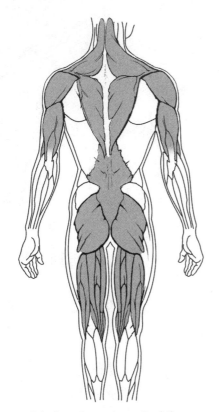

Get fabulous "yoga buns," while you also strengthen your back, with these great exercises.

with no discomfort in your lower back. Postures such as the knee sway, the wheel, the cobra, and the mermaid will help you to keep your spine and lower back healthy. Remember: Your spine is your lifeline. Keep it strong.

In addition to the above-mentioned benefits, the ball—and particularly the band—will also provide important feedback from your body, helping you to feel whether or not you are properly aligned. For example, in the triangle pose, just by holding the band around your upper back, you can feel whether or not your top shoulder is in the correct position, which will help you keep your shoulder from collapsing forward.

In some of the postures, you'll learn how to move on the ball first. Once you get used to doing the posture with the ball, you'll then learn how to incorporate the band. I include the resistance band in the postures where it offers the strongest benefits.

One of the most important parts of yoga is the breathing. Try to stay aware of your breath throughout the yoga pose. Paying attention to your breath not only helps you time the exercise, it will calm and soothe you as well. Breathe in through your nose *and* out through your nose. It takes a little getting used to—but it's very beneficial.

POSE OF THE DANCER

- ▶ **Improves your balance**
- ▶ **Strengthens and tones your legs**
- ▶ **Stretches your chest**
- ▶ **Improves core strength**

The ball will help you to gain your balance in this challenging posture.

A. Stand with the ball about 2 feet in front of you. Place your right palm against the top of the ball. Shift your body weight over your right foot. Exhale as you lift your left foot in toward your buttocks and grasp your left ankle with your left hand. Inhale as you reach back through your left leg, deepening the posture. Hold for 30 seconds, breathing normally, and then release and repeat on the other side.

WARRIOR 1

▶ **Tones your thighs**

▶ **Strengthens your core**

▶ **Stretches your chest, hips, groin, abdomen, and shoulders**

Many people allow their torsos to collapse forward in the warrior 1 pose. Holding the ball overhead will help you keep your torso upright and your chest open, allowing you to feel a deeper stretch in the front of your hips, your abdomen, and your chest.

A. Stand with your feet under your hips. Hold the ball overhead. Exhale as you step forward with your left leg. Inhale and lift your right heel and move it inward so that your rear foot is at a 45-degree angle.

Exhale as you bend your left leg and sink into a deep lunge, as shown. Keep your upper arms in line with your head and reach up and into the ball, as if you were Atlas holding up the world. Hold for 30 seconds, breathing normally. Inhale as you rise to the starting position and then repeat on the other side.

Intermediate Warrior 1

B. Adding the band will help to keep your arms in alignment. Placing the ball under your front leg allows you to sink deeper into the posture. Stand with your feet under your hips. Exhale as you take a large step forward with your left leg. Place the ball under your left thigh. Inhale and lift your right heel and move it inward so that your rear foot is at a 45-degree angle. Grasp the band in both hands and then extend your arms overhead. Exhale as you bend your left knee and sink into the posture, as shown. Feel your left hip come forward as you extend back through your right heel. Hold for 30 seconds, breathing normally. Inhale as you rise and then repeat on the other side.

WARRIOR 2

- ▶ **Tones your thighs**
- ▶ **Strengthens your core**
- ▶ **Stretches your chest, hips, and groin**

The support of the ball under your forward leg allows you to go deeper into this quintessential yoga posture than you ever have before.

A. Stand with your legs in a wide angle and your feet about 3 feet apart. Place the ball just behind your left leg. Turn out your left foot 90 degrees and slide your right heel back slightly. Extend your arms from your shoulders, keeping your shoulders relaxed away from your ears.

Exhale as you bend your left knee, bringing the rear of your thigh onto the top of the ball. Reach back and extend through your right heel, feeling a stretch along the front of your right thigh and hip. Turn your head to look to the left. Breathe normally as you continue to sink into the lunge, holding for 30 seconds. Inhale as you rise to the starting position and then repeat on the other side.

Intermediate Warrior 2

B. Holding an end of your resistance band in each hand will help you keep your arms in proper alignment, helping you to open your chest and extend through your fingertips. Start in the same position with your legs in a wide angle, the ball behind your left leg, and your left foot turned out 90 degrees. Then bring the band around your upper back and grasp an end in each hand. Extend your arms and sink into the posture. The band will pull your arms back slightly, helping you to open your chest.

TRIANGLE

▶ **Stretches your sides, chest, and inner thighs**

▶ **Tones your legs, arms, and torso**

Beginner yoga students often allow their top shoulders to collapse downward in the triangle, reducing the stretch along the sides of their torsos. Using the ball, beginners can easily move into the pose. Because the ball encourages proper body alignment, advanced students may feel more of a stretch when they add it to this posture.

A. Stand with your feet about 3 feet apart. Place the ball underneath your right thigh. Turn your right foot out 90 degrees and slide your left heel back slightly. Extend your arms from your shoulders.

Exhale as you bend to the right, sliding your right hand down your leg as you bend. Extend your left hand toward the ceiling and slightly behind your torso. Turn your head to look up toward the ceiling. Hold for 30 seconds, breathing normally. Inhale as you rise and then repeat on the other side.

Intermediate Triangle

B. Adding the band to the triangle pose will help hold your hands and arms in the proper position, allowing you to feel more of a stretch through your chest. Stand with your feet about 3 feet apart. Place the ball just behind and slightly under your right thigh. Grasp an end of the resistance band in each hand, with the middle of the band around your upper back. With your arms extended, take up the give in the band until it feels taut. Turn your right foot out 90 degrees and slide your left heel back slightly. Extend your arms from your shoulders.

Exhale as you bend to the right. Slide your right hand down your leg as you bend and extend your left hand toward the ceiling. Allow the ball to support your right thigh. Turn your head to look up toward the ceiling. Feel the band gently pulling your hands back and opening your chest. Hold for 30 seconds, breathing normally. Inhale as you rise and then repeat on the other side.

BALANCING STICK

▶ **Improves balance and coordination**

▶ **Tones your abdomen, back, waistline, and legs**

Balancing stick ranks as one of the more challenging postures in yoga. Adding the ball as a prop will help you to hold the posture longer and bring your body into proper alignment.

A. Stand with the ball about 2 feet in front of you. Exhale as you bend forward from your hips, placing your hands against the ball. Raise and extend your left leg.

B. Lift and extend your right arm. Reach out through your right fingertips and left toes to lengthen your spine. Keep your tummy firm as you balance, breathing normally. Keep your head in a neutral position, with your gaze at the floor. Hold for 30 seconds, breathing normally, and then release and repeat on the other side.

MERMAID

▶ **Stretches your sides, chest, neck, and shoulders**

▶ **Strengthens your abdomen**

▶ **Improves your balance**

When you sit on the ball to stretch into the mermaid, you activate your abdominal muscles as they work to keep you stable. The band will help to keep your top shoulder from dropping forward, allowing you to feel a deeper stretch.

A. Sit on the ball with the band between your hips and the ball and with your knees bent and feet on the floor. Grasp one end of the band in your right hand, securing it by your side. Grasp the other end of the band in your left hand, extending your left arm overhead.

B. Exhale as you reach up and over to the right, as shown, feeling the stretch along the left side of your torso. Keep both hips equally planted on the ball. Turn your head to look up. Hold for 30 seconds, breathing normally. Inhale as you rise and then repeat on the other side.

COBRA

- ▶ **Strengthens your back**
- ▶ **Improves your posture**
- ▶ **Stretches your chest**

The ball helps keep your lower back and hips in proper alignment, preventing tightness or pinching in your spine as you extend into the pose. Placing your palms against the front of the ball helps you to extend your spine, allowing you to stretch more deeply.

A. Lie with your tummy on the ball, your legs extended, and the balls of your feet on the floor. Rest your palms on the ball for support.

B. Inhale as you reach through the crown of your head to lengthen your spine as you lift your upper back, neck, and head toward the ceiling. Press your hands into the ball to help lengthen your spine. Hold for 1 minute, breathing normally, and then release.

BRIDGE

Tones your hips, buttocks, thighs, back, and abdomen

Doing the bridge against the ball is a completely different experience than doing it on the floor. With the ball, you'll really feel your hips and buttocks working to keep your torso stable.

A. Sit on the ball with your knees bent at 90 degrees and your feet flat on the floor. Place your palms on the ball for support and slowly walk your feet forward, allowing your back to slide forward along the ball. Release your hands toward the floor and continue to walk your feet out until the ball rests under your shoulders, as shown, supporting your shoulders, neck, and head. Reach your hips toward the ceiling. Hold for 1 minute, breathing normally. Inhale as you walk your feet back in and rise to the starting position.

Intermediate Bridge

B. To increase the challenge of the bridge, extend your arms overhead, making sure to keep your hips up toward the ceiling.

FORWARD BEND

▶ **Stretches the backs of your thighs and your back**

The forward bend is a perfect complement to the wheel, as it brings your spine into the opposite position. Doing it while seated on the ball helps you to tip your pelvis forward as you bend.

A. Sit on the ball. Extend your legs, with your feet about your hips' distance apart.

B. Exhale as you bend forward from your hips and slide your hands down your legs (to your feet, if possible). Try to keep your back long and flat. Hold for 1 minute, breathing normally. Inhale as you rise.

WHEEL

▶ **Stretches your thighs, hips, abdomen, chest, and shoulders**

▶ **Tones your legs and back**

You'll love doing this back bend over the ball. The ball fits snugly into your back, giving you the support you need to extend into the wheel and feel the wonderful, deep stretch along the front of your body. The curve of the ball helps bring your spine into the correct position, preventing pinching between your vertebrae.

A. To bend into the wheel, start by sitting on your ball. Walk your feet forward and bend your knees until your lower back comes in contact with the ball.

B. Extend your legs. Place your palms against the ball for support as you lower your entire torso and head onto the ball. Once your torso is in position, reach back with your hands, as shown, placing your palms on the floor. Hold for 1 minute, breathing normally. Inhale as you release.

THREADING THE NEEDLE

▶ **Stretches your upper back**

▶ **Keeps your spine healthy and strong**

This stretch helps to work the kinks out from between your shoulder blades. I love it.

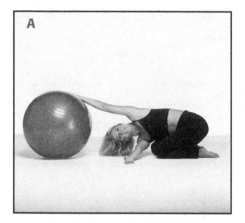

A. Kneel with your hips on top of your heels and shins against the floor. Place both palms on the top of the ball. Reach forward, extending your arms and rolling the ball as far forward as you can without lifting your hips off your heels.

Exhale as you lift your right palm off the ball and slide it under your torso to the left, as shown, as if the space between your body and the floor were the eye of a needle and your arm was the thread. Slide your arm through as far as possible. Then rest the back of your arm against the floor, holding for 30 seconds as you breathe normally. Release and repeat on the other side.

KNEE SWAY

Stretches your spine, lower back, hips, and chest

The ball will help provide a counterstretch, allowing you to create more of a twist in your spine.

A. Lie on your back with your knees in toward your chest. Grasp the ball and extend your arms from your chest.

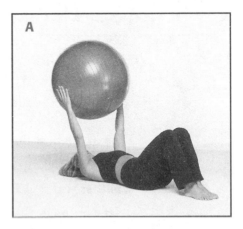

B. Exhale as you lower your knees to the floor to your left and the ball to the floor to the right. Hold for 30 seconds, breathing normally. Inhale as you rise and exhale as you repeat on the opposite side.

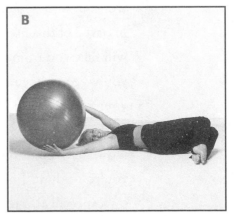

DO-IT-YOURSELF PROGRAMMING

Design your own customized routines

One of the best things about the ball and the band is their portability. Just pick up and go, and they'll travel right along with you, whether you're going to the next room or the next state.

If you have that kind of flexibility and adaptability in your workout tools, you should enjoy them in your workouts as well. In part 3 of this book, you'll find 3 weeks of effective routines that will take you from out of shape to superfit before you know it! If you've gone beyond the 3 weeks, if you'd like to custom-tailor your routine to fit your own preferences, or if you just need a change, you'll find everything you need to know in this chapter. Now that you know the most effective ball and band exercises, you're ready to find out how to mix and match them into your own specially designed, effective routines.

Learning what it takes to pair exercises and create routines allows you to add variety and a personal touch to your program. Variety is the most important key to long-lasting motivation. Keep changing your routine, and you'll never get bored!

My friend and mentor Jack La Lanne, who gave me my start on television in 1981 as his cohost, told me last year that, at age 88, he still changed his workout routine *every month*. It's so important to not let your muscles adapt to your routine. When your muscles can perform your routine by rote, your body burns fewer calories as a result. When you keep your routine fresh, you keep your muscles constantly guessing. So change it up every month for maximum fat-burning, flexibility, and fitness.

THE ELEMENTS OF YOUR SUCCESS

The only way you can begin to achieve your dreams is to know what they are. Before you can design any routine, or mix and match routines into a customized program, you first must establish a goal. Although your main goal may be to lose weight, you must set three mini goals to get there. I suggest that you make it your goal to improve your:

- ▸ Flexibility through stretching
- ▸ Strength, balance, and coordination through toning exercises with the stability ball and bands
- ▸ Cardiovascular endurance with fat-burning "cardio" (also called aerobic) exercise

These components are essential to a well-balanced fitness program. If you leave out any one of these three crucial elements—stretching, toning, and cardio—you might not see results as quickly.

For example, if you do *only* cardiovascular exercise, eventually your joints will begin to feel stiff from the lack of stretching. Your muscles may still be flabby. Similarly, if you perform *only* toning moves, omitting cardio and stretching, you will also feel soreness in your joints and tightness in your muscles. You will also miss out on the wonderful fat-burning ability that comes from cardio exercise and will need to eat much less food to lose weight and keep it off. Plus, you won't condition your heart and lungs and therefore may miss out on the endurance, energy, and disease-preventing benefits that come from cardiovascular exercise.

To include all three elements in your program, you need not spend an inordinate amount of time exercising. To the contrary, you can work all three into a comprehensive program within a minimum of time. I personally can do it all in an efficient 30-minute workout. Throughout this chapter, you'll learn how to make your program quick and effective. First, however, select the type of cardio exercise you will do.

DESIGN YOUR BEST CARDIO PROGRAM

To become truly fit and healthy, you must do some type of cardiovascular exercise that gets your heart pumping, such as running, walking, biking, swimming, or rowing. Your cardio routine will do much more than help you burn off excess fat. Research shows that regular doses of cardio exercise help to regulate your appetite, helping you automatically stop eating once your body no longer needs calories. Cardio also conditions your heart and lungs, boosts your immune system, and helps prevent disease. Cardio improves blood flow through your arteries and even encourages your body to build new capillaries. Because your blood carries energizing oxygen and nutrients to every cell in your body, cardio also gives you more stamina for everyday life. Finally, many people, myself included, get a wonderful mood boost from cardiovascular exercise. I consider it a natural medicine for the mind.

Aim for 3 or 4 days of cardio each week. Depending on your goals, you can perform anywhere from 12 to 60 minutes of cardio during each session. Twelve minutes is the bare minimum amount of time that will produce results. The more minutes you add, the more calories you'll burn. I personally aim for more than 30 minutes of cardio 4 days a week. I like to incorporate different types of cardio over the course of the week. Some days I'll walk with my girlfriends. Other days I'll do aerobics at home with one of my videos. Sometimes I run on the treadmill or work out on an elliptical machine. Including lots of variety by constantly changing your cardio routine helps you target different muscle groups, increase your fat burning, and boost your motivation.

Now that you know how *long* you want to exercise, let's take a closer look at *how* you will exercise. Many people ask me, "Denise, what's the best form of cardio for weight loss?"

I answer, "The type of cardio that you will do."

No matter what type of cardiovascular exercise you choose, as long as you get your heart rate up, you're reaping the wonderful benefits of this form of exercise.

PICK YOUR CARDIO LEVEL

Consult the following chart to determine the right amount of cardio exercise for you.

Level	Time Commitment	Best for . . .
1	12 minutes	People new to exercise who want to shape up with only a minimum amount of time spent exercising
2	24 minutes	People with a regular exercise routine who want to lose more than 5 pounds
3	36 minutes	People with a regular exercise routine who want to lose more than 10 pounds
4	48 minutes	People with a regular exercise routine who want to get in top shape for a special occasion, such as a wedding or high school reunion
5	60 minutes	Athletes who love fitness, have plenty of time to spend on fitness, and enjoy the challenge of getting their bodies in optimal shape (I usually try to fit in my 60-minute sessions on the weekends with my husband.)

When deciding what form of exercise to tackle, I suggest that you pay less attention to the amount of calories that each type of cardiovascular exercise burns, and more to how you personally feel about each type of exercise. The type of exercise you enjoy the most is the type that you will do consistently. Consistency is one important key to your success.

Let's look at the different benefits you'll get from each of several types of cardiovascular exercise.

$\left\{\begin{array}{c}\text{"The best type of cardiovascular exercise}\\\text{is that type you will do most often."}\end{array}\right\}$

Walking. If you're a beginner, this is a great cardio choice, because you need minimal equipment and expertise. Also, most people are able to walk without discomfort—a big plus that will help you keep your long-term commitment to exercise. I love to walk for fitness.

Jogging/running. Jogging burns more calories per minute than walking, making it a wonderfully efficient fat-burning workout. To slowly progress from walking to jogging, add a 1-minute jogging burst for each 10 minutes of walking. Once you can do that, add 2 minutes, and then 3, until eventually you are jogging for 9 minutes with just 1 minute of walking.

Swimming and water aerobics. If you have arthritis, bad knees, a bad back, or any type of pain in general, the pool can be your best friend. Water takes weight off your body, allowing you to move pain-free.

Bike riding. Whether you're on a stationary, Spinning, or road bike, cycling provides a great calorie-burning workout. It's also easy on the knees. If you have a bad back or are overweight, consider buying a recumbent bike, which allows you to lean back as you pedal.

Jumping rope. This very challenging, efficient, calorie-incinerating workout is perfect for people who can't exercise outdoors because of the weather or safety concerns but who also have limited space indoors for movement. If you have trouble coordinating your arms with your feet, start by jumping without the rope, and then add the rope later. For variety, try jumping jacks, small jumps, large jumps, and jogging with the rope.

Stairclimbing, elliptical, and other cardio machines. Whether you use them at home or at the gym, exercise machines can make working out much more convenient. Maybe you'll like to watch television to distract yourself as you work out on the stairclimber, the treadmill, or the rowing machine. These machines also allow you to exercise indoors during bad weather.

Cardio on the ball. Yes, you can even complete your cardio workout on the ball—it's that versatile! No other type of exercise equipment has this kind of range.

A close friend of mine, Lisa Wheeler, teaches an entire class in New York City designed around cardio on the ball. In her classes, she has the students do everything from sitting and bouncing on the ball, to ball taps (see page 62), tummy tucks (see page 46), and ball jacks (which are basically bouncing jumping jacks from a seated position on the ball).

With a little imagination, you can incorporate the ball into any traditional aerobic-dance move. And with a little more imagination, you'll be able to dream up a whole slew of cardio-on-the-ball options. On the following pages, you'll find four of my favorites. Put on some fun music and just go! You can do these movements as your official cardio for the day, running through and repeating the series as necessary until you've amassed 12, 24, or more cardio minutes. You can also intersperse these moves into your toning routine, creating a fun circuit workout that will keep your heart rate up the entire time.

HEEL TAPS

▶ **Rev up your heart rate**

▶ **Warm up your legs**

Heel taps come from aerobics. Holding the ball out in front will help incorporate your upper body into this quintessential aerobic-dance movement.

A. Stand with your feet under your hips. Hold the ball at chest level. Bend your knees and extend your left leg, tapping your heel to the floor in front of you. As you do so, extend your arms, reaching the ball forward.

B. Return both your foot and the ball to the starting position and then repeat with the other leg, alternating back and forth.

STEP AND REACH

► **Revs up your heart rate**

► **Warms up your legs**

As you squat down and pivot from side to side, you must use your arms to move the ball up and down, using your entire body. This will get your heart rate up!

A. Stand with your feet under your hips. Hold the ball at chest level. Bend your knees and squat down. Then lift the ball up and over to the left as you bring your body weight over to your left leg, as shown, and lift your extended right leg off the floor.

B. Lower the ball, bring both feet to the floor, and bend your knees, as shown. Then step and reach over to the right.

DIZZY BALL

▶ **Improves coordination**

▶ **Revs up your heart rate**

Do you remember playing dizzy bats as a child? You would place one hand on top of a bat and spin around it as many times as you could before you collapsed into fits of laughter. This exercise is just as fun!

A. Place the ball in the center of the room. Stand as far away from the ball as you can, given the size of the room. Run over to the ball, place one hand on top of it, run a complete circle around it, and then race back to your starting position.

B. Run back to the ball and place your other hand on it, circling the ball in the opposite direction.

JOGGING ATLAS

▶ **Revs up your metabolism**

▶ **Warms up your legs and arms**

You can march or jog for this one. Pretend that the ball is the planet and you are Atlas, in charge of holding it up!

A. Stand with your feet under your hips. Hold the ball with your arms extended overhead. March or jog in place.

{ "Doesn't this make you feel powerful?" }

No matter what type of cardio you decide to do, always include a warmup and a cooldown, each 2 to 5 minutes long. Your warmup will slowly increase your heart rate, getting more blood to your muscles to ready them for your workout. Your cooldown will allow your heart to slow down gradually. To either warm up or cool down, just go a little more slowly than usual. For example, if you're walking, start at a leisurely pace for a few minutes and then pick up the pace by pumping your arms.

DESIGNING YOUR ROUTINES

Now that you've chosen your duration and type of cardio, you're ready for the most important piece of the training puzzle: how to design individual toning routines.

To make your routines as efficient as possible, you'll probably want to order your exercises in such a way that you can move quickly from one exercise to another without taking a break. Usually, when you work a muscle—let's say, for example, your chest muscle—you should let that muscle rest for about a minute so it can re-

GO FOR THE EXTRA CREDIT

I never miss an opportunity to move. I call these little 1-minute exercise bursts "fidget-cisers," and I truly rely on them to help keep me trim and toned, particularly when I know I'll be spending much of the day on the phone. Here are some examples of what I like to do.

▶ Standing leg lifts as I blow-dry my hair

▶ Marching in place as I talk on the phone

▶ Taking the stairs instead of the elevator every chance I get

▶ Curling the grocery bags as I carry them in from the car

▶ Squeezing my buttocks muscles as I stand in line

cover before you attempt another exercise for that body area. This is one reason that you often see gym-goers sitting around staring into space. They are waiting for the muscle they just worked to recover so they can complete another set.

Who has this kind of time? It's not an efficient way to exercise. If you had to rest for a minute between each of your 12 moves, your session would last 24 minutes instead of 12!

The good news is that if you pay attention to the sequence of your exercises, you don't need to rest between movements. In order to move from one exercise into the next without a break, you have three options.

1. Work while you rest. With some planning, you can allow the muscle you just worked to rest while you target an opposing, or opposite, muscle on your body. For example, you could work your chest, and then quickly move on to an upper-back exercise, and then move back to your chest.

Opposing muscles are the ones that stretch as their opposite muscle contracts. As you contract your biceps to do a biceps curl, the opposing muscle, your triceps, relaxes and stretches. Similarly, when you target the fronts of your thighs, the backs of your thighs relax and stretch. Working opposing muscle groups does more than help you save time—it also helps you to sculpt your muscles in a balanced manner. By working your opposing muscles equally you can avoid the strength imbalances that tend to lead to injuries.

2. Take a giant leap. You can also efficiently work one body area by doing supersets, two or three exercises for that body area without a break. For example, you might do chest presses and chest flies one after the other. By the time you move on to the chest flies, you may not be able to do as many repetitions as if you started out with them. When you finish the superset, however, you'll have worked your entire chest area thoroughly—and you'll feel it!

3. Flow smoothly from standing to sitting. One of my quirks is that I don't like to stand up and sit down and get back up again. It somehow ruins the flow of the workout for me. So I like to start my routines with exercises in a standing position, move on to the ones in a sitting position, and finish with the ones I do while lying down. I work opposite muscle groups and do supersets as needed so I can continue to flow through the series without a break.

To put exercises together into a complete set of 12, first decide on your goal for the session. Do you plan to zero in on a particular body area, such as your upper or lower body? Do you want to work your entire body at once? Do want to do a separate form of cardio, or would you rather create a circuit workout that will simultaneously tone your muscles and get your heart rate up?

Once you know your goal, skim down to the appropriate section to learn how to put movements together.

Designing an Upper-Body Routine

Your upper-body routine should target the major muscles in your upper body.

- ▸ Chest (pectoralis major)
- ▸ Upper back (rhomboids, lats, and trapezius)
- ▸ Shoulders (deltoids)
- ▸ Arms (biceps and triceps)

SAMPLE BEGINNER UPPER-BODY ROUTINE

1. Chest stretch (page 130)
2. Chest press (page 86)
3. Chest firmer (page 90)
4. Arm row (page 92)
5. Upper-back toner (page 98)
6. Lateral raise (page 94)
7. Front raise (page 96)
8. Biceps curl (page 108)
9. Hammer curl (page 110)
10. Triceps kickback (page 104)
11. French curl (page 106)
12. Arm stretch (page 131)

Generally, you'll want to work your larger muscles first, which means doing the exercises for your chest and upper back before working your shoulders and arms.

To design your routine, choose:

▸ Two chest exercises (chest press, page 86; pushup, page 88; chest firmer, page 90)

▸ Two upper-back exercises (upper-back firmer, page 91; arm row, page 92; upper-back toner, page 98; upright row, page 100; lat pulldown, page 111; Pilates rowing series, page 150)

▸ Two shoulder exercises (lateral raise, page 94; front raise, page 96; back and shoulder firmer, page 99; overhead press, page 102; the bug, page 139)

▸ Two triceps exercises (triceps kickback, page 104; arm firmer, page 105; French curl, page 106; Pilates rowing series, page 150)

▸ Two biceps exercises (biceps curl, page 108; hammer curl, page 110)

Once you pick 10 upper-body moves, pick two upper-body stretches from chapters 6 and 8. Do one stretch as a warmup and the other either in the middle or at the end of the routine.

SAMPLE INTERMEDIATE UPPER-BODY ROUTINE

1. Upper-back stretch (page 116)
2. Advanced chest press (page 87)
3. Pushup (page 88)
4. Upper-back firmer (page 91)
5. Intermediate arm row (page 92)
6. Intermediate upright row (page 101)
7. Back and shoulder firmer (page 99)
8. Intermediate biceps curl (page 109)
9. Hammer curl (page 110)
10. Arm firmer (page 105)
11. Intermediate French curl (page 107)
12. Shoulder stretch (page 128)

Designing a Lower-Body Routine

To shrink and sculpt your lower half, you must target your hips, thighs, and buttocks from every angle. This means including exercises that target:

- ▸ The fronts of the thighs (quadriceps)
- ▸ The backs of the thighs (hamstrings)
- ▸ Outsides of the thighs and hips (abductors)
- ▸ Inner thighs (adductors)
- ▸ Buttocks (gluteals)

To design your routine, choose:

- ▸ One exercise for the fronts of the thighs (quad sets, page 76)
- ▸ Two exercises for the outer thighs (outer-thigh toner, page 69; front/back, page 141; hip circles, page 142)
- ▸ Two exercises for the inner thighs (ball squeeze, page 67; inner-thigh shaper, page 81)
- ▸ Two exercises for the backs of the thighs and buttocks (hamstring curl, page 64; bottoms-up, page 66; butt and thigh firmer, page 70; deadlift, page 71; back-of-thigh toner, page 74; hip slimmer, page 80)

SAMPLE BEGINNER LOWER-BODY ROUTINE

1. Thigh stretch (page 119)
2. Wall squat (page 60)
3. Hip slimmer (page 80)
4. Thigh blaster (page 58)
5. Quad sets (page 76)
6. Hip stretch (page 125)
7. Hamstring stretch (page 126)
8. Outer-thigh toner (page 69)
9. Inner-thigh shaper (page 81)
10. Butt and thigh firmer (page 70)
11. Bottoms-up (page 66)
12. Ball squeeze (page 67)

▶ Three exercises that target multiple lower-body muscles (thigh blaster, page 58; wall squat, page 60; ball tap, page 62; floor tap, page 63; lower-body toner, page 68; lunge, page 72; leg lunge, page 73; thigh shaper, page 78; leg circles with band, page 82; leg circles with ball, page 147; warrior 1, page 156; warrior 2, page 158; triangle, page 160)

Then pick two lower-body stretches from chapters 6 and 8. Do one stretch at the beginning of the routine and the other one either in the middle or at the end of the routine.

Designing Routines for the Core: Abs, Back, and Waistline

To flatten your tummy, shrink your waistline, and help keep your back healthy and pain-free, you must work every aspect of your core. It's all about balance.

In order to work your entire core, your exercises must target:

▶ The lower tummy, below the navel (lower rectus abdominis)

▶ The upper tummy, above the navel (upper rectus abdominis)

▶ The sides of your waist (obliques)

▶ The deepest tummy muscle (transverse abdominis)

▶ The lower back

SAMPLE INTERMEDIATE LOWER-BODY ROUTINE

1. Triangle (page 160)

2. Warrior 1 (page 156)

3. Floor tap (page 63)

4. Thigh stretch (page 119)

5. Hip slimmer (page 80)

6. Thigh shaper (page 78)

7. Quad sets (page 76)

8. Hamstring stretch (page 126)

9. Outer-thigh toner (page 69)

10. Hamstring curl (page 64)

11. Intermediate hamstring curl (page 65)

12. Advanced ball squeeze (page 67)

To design your routine, choose:

- ▸ Two exercises for the lower tummy (pelvic tilt, page 34; lower-tummy firmer, page 41; ultimate tummy trimmer, page 47; bicycle, page 48; roll-down, page 144; double-leg stretch, page 148)

- ▸ Two for the upper tummy (traditional crunch, page 36; tummy flattener, page 42)

- ▸ Two for the obliques and waistline (oblique twist, page 38; waistline trimmer, page 43; Pilates twist, page 137; saw, page 138; T-stand, page 140)

- ▸ Two core exercises (torso toner, page 40; plank, page 44; Pilates tummy tuck, page 136; Pilates plank, page 143; teaser, page 146; balancing stick, page 162; bridge, page 165)

- ▸ Two exercises for the lower back (natural tummy tuck, page 46; back toner, page 50; lower-back strengthener, page 51; rise and shine, page 52; reciprocal reach, page 54)

- ▸ One abdominal stretch (hip release, page 124; cobra, page 164; wheel, page 167)

SAMPLE BEGINNER CORE ROUTINE

1. Hug-a-ball (page 115)
2. Traditional crunch (page 36)
3. Tummy flattener (page 42)
4. Torso toner (page 40)
5. Back stretch (page 35)
6. Plank (page 44)
7. Back toner (page 50)
8. Reciprocal reach (page 54)
9. Waistline trimmer (page 43)
10. T-stand (page 140)
11. Lower-tummy firmer (page 41)
12. Pelvic tilt (page 34)

> { "The more muscles you incorporate into your workout, the more calories you burn." }

▶ One lower-back stretch (back stretch, page 35; waist rotation/lower-back stretch, page 117; spine stretch, page 120; child's pose, page 132; knee sway, page 169)

Designing Routines for the Total Body

You'll find numerous total-body routines every Monday, Wednesday, and Friday in the 3-week program in part 3. Week 1 contains beginner options, week 2 is more intermediate, and week 3 is just a bit more challenging, to make the most of your advances from the first 2 weeks.

To design your own total-body routine, choose:

▶ Four upper-body moves (see "Designing an Upper-Body Routine" on page 182)

▶ Four lower-body moves (see "Designing a Lower-Body Routine" on page 184)

SAMPLE INTERMEDIATE CORE ROUTINE

1. Pilates tummy tuck (page 136)
2. Intermediate crunch (page 37)
3. Advanced oblique twist (page 39)
4. Back stretch (page 35)
5. Intermediate Pilates plank (page 143)
6. Intermediate rise and shine (page 52)
7. Lower-back strengthener (page 51)
8. T-stand (page 140)
9. Teaser (page 146)
10. Intermediate bicycle (page 49)
11. Lower-tummy firmer (page 41)
12. Double-leg stretch (page 148)

- ▸ Two core moves (see "Designing Routines for the Core: Abs, Back, and Waistline" on page 185)
- ▸ One stretch (see chapter 6)

You can also add in some cardio on the ball to keep your heart rate up. To do so, add in a cardio-on-the-ball move between every two or three toning moves.

DESIGNING YOUR WEEKLY PROGRAM

Now that you know how to put your own customized routines together, it's time to learn how to work those routines into a typical week. I recommend that you exercise 6 days a week, even if some of the days include only a 12-minute workout. Your complete plan should include:

- ▸ 3 to 4 days of cardio, lasting 12 to 60 minutes per session
- ▸ 3 to 5 days of toning, lasting 12 minutes per routine
- ▸ 1 day of stretching, lasting 12 minutes per routine

SAMPLE CIRCUIT WORKOUT

1. Pilates tummy tuck (page 136)
2. Jogging Atlas (page 179)
3. Chest press (page 86)
4. Front raise (page 96)
5. Dizzy ball (page 178)
6. Upper-back toner (page 98)
7. Biceps curl (page 108)
8. Triceps kickback (page 104)
9. Heel taps (page 176)
10. Thigh blaster (page 58)
11. Ball squeeze (page 67)
12. Bottoms-up (page 66)
13. Hamstring curl (page 64)
14. Step and reach (page 177)
15. Torso toner (page 40)
16. Plank (page 44)
17. Jogging Atlas (page 179)

If you'd like, you can combine your cardio, toning, and stretching into one session to save time. For example, this morning I ran 2 miles on my treadmill and then did a 12-minute ball and band toning routine for the upper body that included some stretches. I was done within 30 minutes, I had covered all my bases, and I felt great.

To organize your weekly program, follow the general rule that you must give your muscles a day of rest between toning sessions to allow them to repair themselves and grow stronger. That doesn't mean, however, that you can work out only every other day. If you do an upper-body routine on a Monday, for example, you can do an abdominal or lower-body routine on a Tuesday. Similarly, if you design a routine that works your entire body, then you'll tone just 3 days a week and use the remaining days to add to your cardio routine.

What you schedule into your sample week depends on your interests and goals. For example, if your body is well-proportioned and you want to firm up and slim down, the following schedule will work for you.

Monday: Upper-body routine; cardio

Tuesday: Lower-body routine

Wednesday: Abdominal routine; cardio

Thursday: Cardio

Friday: Total-body cardio circuit

Saturday: Stretching

Sunday: Day off

On the other hand, if you want to give your hips, thighs, and buttocks some extra attention, you might design your week this way.

Monday: Hips, thighs, and buttocks routine

Tuesday: Upper-body and core cardio circuit

Wednesday: Hips, thighs, and buttocks routine

Thursday: Upper-body and core cardio circuit

Friday: Hips, thighs, and buttocks routine

Saturday: Stretching

Sunday: Day off

Finally, if you want to give your midsection some extra attention, your weekly schedule might look like this.

Monday: Abs, back, and waistline routine

Tuesday: Upper-body and lower-body cardio circuit

Wednesday: Abs, back, and waistline routine

Thursday: Upper-body and lower-body cardio circuit

Friday: Abs, back, and waistline routine

Saturday: Stretching

Sunday: Day off

Now that you know how to design your own customized routine, you have the tools to make your ball and band a part of your fitness plan for life—you'll never get bored and, more important, neither will your muscles. Before you start tinkering around with all your options, you can get your new program going with a turbocharged, 3-week jump start. Just turn to part 3 and start shedding pounds and sculpting your body the fastest, most effective way possible!

PART 3

YOUR 3-WEEK PLAN

WEEK 1

Welcome to your 3-week plan—and congratulations on making the commitment to becoming fit, slim, and healthy!

This 3-week progressive plan starts at the beginner level and allows you to build fitness gradually. Have faith in your abilities and charge full speed ahead into the program with confidence. I know you can do it. I want *you* to know that as well. Right now, say to yourself out loud, "I can do it!"

I've designed this 3-week plan with efficiency in mind. If you are a person who leads a busy life and feels as if you don't have a moment to spare, this is the program for you. It requires a minimum amount of time for toning—just 12 minutes a day, 5 days a week. Your 12-minute workouts may be short on time, but they're big on results. You'll fit in walking or another form of cardio around those toning routines, committing yourself to an amount of time ranging from as little as 12 minutes of your favorite high-energy exercise to a nice, rejuvenating hour-long stroll, depending on your lifestyle and goals. You'll combine this with a healthful eating plan that includes quick and easy meals. Losing weight and keeping it off have never taken less time!

To clinch your success on the 3-week plan, you'll focus on

five simple keys: healthful eating, sculpting and stretching routines, cardio, water, and rest.

QUICK AND EASY MEALS FOR WEIGHT LOSS

Every day on your plan, you'll savor delicious meals from a complete menu plan that's perfectly balanced—you'll get the optimal amount of important nutrients for health while enjoying each bite and feeling incredibly satisfied. Each meal is quick and easy to prepare, so you'll spend more time savoring and less time slaving! Believe me, you'll love how quick and easy it will be to put a great meal on the table for yourself and your whole family. When I'm feeling really pressed for time, it's great to know that I can still cook a wholesome meal for my family that will also help keep me trim.

Ace nutritionist Leslie Bonci, R.D., helped design these menus, which take advantage of all the latest research to help you lose weight and keep it off. These menus focus on delicious, healthful meals that you can cook quickly—almost every one can be completed within 12 minutes. (And the ones that take a bit longer employ the oven, not the stove, so you can walk away!) Your menu options include a healthful balance of lean protein, fiber, fat, and good-quality carbohydrates.

Remember when, not too long ago, high-carbohydrate, low-fat diets were very popular? We've since learned that scaling back too much on protein and fat can backfire, causing you to feel hungry, triggering cravings, and, eventually, promoting weight gain.

But this doesn't mean that I'm a fan of high-protein diets. Rather, I'm a big believer in nutritional balance. I believe in fresh, wholesome meals that balance all of the macronutrients—protein, fat, and carbohydrate. Leslie and I have chosen the best, freshest foods to get plenty of each food group in these weight-loss menus: the leanest of meats and fish for protein; healthy plant-based fats from flaxseeds, avocados, nuts, and olive oil; and crunchy vegetables, fruit, and minimally processed grains for carbohydrate.

"Even carbs?" you may be asking yourself. Sure! Carbs—the right carbs—are a very important component of nutrition. They give us energy to think clearly, to get the most out of our workouts, and to power us through our days. And let's face it: Carbs are often downright yummy. When people go on restrictive no-carb diets, they often just lose their desire to eat. That's no life, and it's certainly not a healthy, long-term plan. We've selected the right carbs, in the right proportions, to help you not only reach your weight-loss goals but also stay energized and satisfied.

You will never feel hungry on this eating plan. At every meal, you'll fill up on satisfying fiber, protein, or both. Studies show that the fiber you get from vegetables, beans, fruit, and whole grains is very important to help you slow digestion and steady your blood sugar levels. Fiber also tempers your appetite, helping you to fill up on fewer calories. Protein does the same—your body breaks down protein much more slowly than it does carbohydrate. For example, when you eat a plain bagel, you may feel hungry just an hour or two later, even though you just ate 400 calories. But when you eat just half of a whole wheat bagel with a slice of smoked salmon on top—totaling fewer calories—the protein in the salmon and the fiber from the whole grains will keep you satisfied longer.

Being satisfied after you eat isn't just about feeling full—you also have to offer your tastebuds something delicious. The fats in these menus allow you to indulge your culinary senses. Again, it's all about making the right choices. Eating the right fat can help eliminate those feelings of deprivation that can lead to late-night refrigerator raids. The fats I've included in the 3-week-plan menus are all good for your health and for your waistline. You'll scale back on the unhealthful fats—the trans fats and saturated fats found in commercially baked goods, many processed foods, fried food, and most animal products. At the same time, you'll increase your consumption of the healthful fats, including the omega-3 and omega-6 fatty acids found in plant foods (flaxseeds, olives, avocados, and nuts), fish, and vegetable oils (olive oil). Research shows that a diet rich in these healthful fats promotes heart health, reduces the risk of cancer, lifts depression, soothes joint pain, and, yes, even helps you lose weight.

As you go through the menus, feel free to modify by substituting your favorite fruits and vegetables, or different protein or grain choices. The portion sizes are listed, so just fill in with your preferred foods. Remember, if you don't like it, you won't enjoy it, and you'll be looking for something else to fill the void.

SCULPTING AND STRETCHING EVERY MUSCLE

Toning your body has never been simpler. You'll complete your 12-minute toning routines during the week, Monday through Friday. These routines will tone your upper, middle, and lower body in a balanced way, shrinking and shaping your arms, shoulders, back, tummy, waistline, hips, thighs, and buttocks. On Mondays, Wednesdays, and Fridays, your 12-minute routine emphasizes the upper and lower body. On Tuesdays and Thursdays, you will zero in on your abs, back, and waistline. I've incorporated stretches into each routine, so you can simultaneously lengthen your muscles as you strengthen them—another way you'll be making the most of these efficient exercises.

Each Saturday, you will complete a gentle stretching routine that will help rejuvenate your body, encourage muscle recovery from the previous 5 days, and give your body some tender loving care.

As you move through the 3-week program, the toning routines will become slightly more difficult, challenging your fitness and encouraging consistent, efficient results. If you ever find an exercise too challenging, return to the beginner or intermediate level. Listen to your body at all times. Be careful not to challenge yourself beyond your limits or, worse yet, to go through the motions and fail to reach your limits! Try to find the fine line between pushing your body just a little past its comfort zone and pushing your body into your *dis*comfort zone.

FAT-BURNING CARDIO

To burn that butter, you need to get your heart pumping, too! You'll work cardio into your routine 3 or 4 days a week, starting with 12-minute sessions and building up to your personal fitness goal. (See "Pick Your Cardio Level" on page 173 to help you determine how much time you'll spend exercising aerobically.)

You want to become truly fit, so you need to do some type of cardiovascular—"cardio"—exercise that gets your blood charging through your veins. Your cardio routine is terrific at helping you burn off fat, condition your heart and lungs, stay healthy, and prevent disease. It will also boost your mood and energy, making you happier and more likely to stay away from emotional eating. I recommend power-walking because it's the most convenient form of cardio around, but pick a cardio option that works for you. Depending on your lifestyle, it might be running, walking, biking, swimming, rowing, even climbing the stairs of your office building—as long as you get your heart rate up, you're doing it right! (See chapter 9 for a list of cardio options and their benefits.)

Complete your cardio sessions at a time that best works into your schedule. You may get up in the morning, warm up with cardio, and then launch into your toning routine. Or, you may choose to do your toning in the morning and your cardio after work. You may also split up your cardio, performing some of your time in the morning and adding in more time throughout the day in the form of short cardio bursts. All of these methods are equally effective! The choice is yours. Choose the method that best fits into your schedule.

WATER WHISKS AWAY POUNDS

Water is one of your body's best friends. You need water for countless processes, from food digestion to body-temperature regulation. Even though water contains no calories, it helps contribute to a feeling of fullness, especially when you drink it right before your meals. Because your brain and blood are largely made of water, a shortfall can make you feel tired, sluggish, and dull. I try to drink eight 8- to 12-ounce glasses of water a day. As soon as I wake up in the morning, I go straight to the kitchen and down two glasses of water at the sink. After 8 hours of sleep, our bodies are dehydrated, and they need water to help get all systems in gear and burning at peak efficiency. I also find that if I drink a glass before each meal and one with meals, it automatically helps me eat less. Making water my main liquid staple helps me avoid other drinks, such as soft drinks or juice drinks that contain hidden calories.

REST REBUILDS YOUR MUSCLES

Sleep is heavenly, and as a culture, we need more of it. You see, rest is just as important to your body as movement. As you sleep, your body secretes the hormones responsible for repairing and strengthening your muscles. Research has found over and over again that people who routinely skimp on their sleep tend to age faster than those who get in a full 8 hours—yet it's often the first thing we women are tempted to cut short when time is tight! When you chronically deprive yourself of the rest you need, your metabolism slows, your muscles start to ache, your fitness plan results drop off, and your energy levels plummet. Try this: Just like you do with your kids, decide on a set bedtime and make a firm commitment to get yourself to bed on time. And don't forget—if you set your alarm 15 minutes earlier to fit in a morning workout, make sure to go to bed 15 minutes earlier at night.

SCULPTING YOUR BEST BODY

You'll kick off your 3-week plan on a Sunday. During your first day on the plan, you will complete no official exercise nor follow an official menu. Instead, you'll use the day to prepare for the weeks ahead by:

- ▶ Stepping on the scale and taking your measurements
- ▶ Setting a goal
- ▶ Shopping for the food you'll need and preparing a few items in advance
- ▶ Making sure you have your equipment (stability ball and resistance bands) and workout space ready for action

I'm so excited for you. You will soon learn how to combine good nutrition, fat-burning cardio, toning and stretching, plenty of water, and plenty of rest to make over your body, your mind, and your life. You'll become the healthiest and happiest that you can be, and you'll create a balanced body, mind, and soul. In just 21 days, you'll be well on your way to sculpting a new you—a you who is open to new possibilities, a you who is balanced, strong, flexible, coordinated, and, most important, successful and satisfied.

day 1
(Sunday)

DENISE'S DAILY WISDOM

Many of my fans ask me whether I think it's a good idea to work a "cheat day" into their week. On the cheat day, they would eat all of the foods they love in large portions and toss self-discipline aside. Then, for the other 6 days of the week, they would return to an extremely healthful way of eating.

Although this approach certainly works for some people, I find it backfires for most. Many people tell me that one cheat day turns into two and then three. Suddenly, anytime they feel a craving, they declare it a cheat day. To stick to a new, healthful way of eating, most people—myself included—must regularly indulge in the foods they love.

When I feel like having ice cream—and my kids do, too—I try to eat just one scoop. I enjoy the ice cream without going overboard. Just remember to dish up reasonable portions. I recommend you follow the 80/20 rule—make 80 percent of your foods healthy. The other 20 percent can be fun foods that you love. Once you allow yourself to eat the foods you love, you no longer have to cheat. Your cravings diminish, and you return to a sensible way of eating that results in permanent weight loss.

{ "Start moving your body, and your mind and motivation will follow." }

day

(1) THE DAILY DOZEN

Day Off!

You will do no official exercise today. Instead, you'll spend some time getting ready for the exciting week ahead. I've found that when starting a new program, preparation—both in your body and your mind—can be *way* more than half the battle. If you can get yourself off to a good start by anticipating any challenges to your program, you're almost guaranteed to succeed!

Weigh-In

To be able to enjoy how much your body will change in 3 weeks, you'll want to have an accurate picture of where you began. Take a moment to jot down the following information in a notebook or journal.

- ▸ Your current weight
- ▸ Your current waist, bust, hips, thighs, and arm measurements
- ▸ Your current clothing size

And, if available:

- ▸ Your current body-fat percentage
- ▸ Your current health statistics (cholesterol level, glucose level, and so forth)

Reflection

At the end of each week, you'll take a moment to reflect on your accomplishments and challenges. Today's reflection will help you to anticipate future challenges. Answer these questions in your notebook.

1. What personal strengths can you call upon to help you stick with the program?

2. What personal challenges must you anticipate? How will you overcome these challenges?

3. What one goal do you plan to accomplish in the coming week? (For example: plan to get up 5 minutes earlier, give up eating past 7:00 P.M., or some other small, measurable step that will help you achieve your goals.)

Preparation

A few moments of preparation today will make the rest of the week's plan come together quickly and easily. First and foremost, make sure that you have the right size and resistance of ball and bands (see chapter 2 for guidance in choosing the best one for you) and that you've selected a time and place to exercise. On page 293, you'll find a shopping list of the items you'll need for the week's quick and easy menus and recipes. Shop for these items today, then quickly scan the menus to see if there's anything you could do ahead of time—like slice up some peppers, prepare broccoli florets, or cut up celery sticks for handy snacking—to make your cooking time even faster. Nearly every meal is designed to be completed in 12 minutes or less.

{ I DID IT! } ▸

Name: Stephanie O'Reilly

Age: 31

Town: San Luis Obispo, California

Weight Lost: 50 pounds

Other Accomplishments: Shrank from a size 18 to a size 14

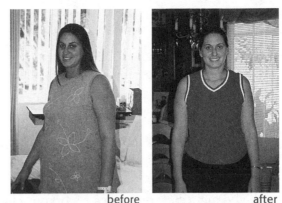

before   after

"With Denise's help, I've shrunk from a size 18 to a size 14 and lost 50 pounds in 9 months! I discovered Denise after I gave birth in November 2002. I wanted to get back to my prepregnancy size and shape as soon as possible, so I purchased a number of her videos and exercised to them or her Lifetime television show almost every day. On the days that I didn't exercise with Denise, I power-walked 4 miles. Each week, I noticed my body grow stronger, leaner, and firmer. In just 9 months, I lost all of the baby weight.

"Each morning when I turn on the TV and see Denise, I feel motivated and happy to see her. On the weekends, when her show doesn't air, I do one of her videos. I have 16 of Denise's videos, and I love them all! I have found yoga and Pilates—on or off the ball—to be wonderful stress relievers. These routines create time for me to get in touch with my body.

"I now have more energy to chase my 9-month-old around the house. Before I lost the weight, a lot of women told me that they doubted I could get back in shape after having a baby. I believed in Denise Austin, and I proved them wrong! She is an inspiration to me. I did it!"

Stephanie's Advice: Make exercise routine. Do it every day at the same time, and it will become a habit. To motivate yourself, keep a photo of yourself when you were fit and happy in a place where it will help you when you most need it, such as on the refrigerator door or by the alarm clock. It will help keep you focused on your goal.

DENISE'S DAILY WISDOM

For many people, morning is not only the best time to exercise, it's the only time. When everyone else is still in bed, you can get up and do your Daily Dozen routine without feeling rushed and without interruption. Over the years, my fans have told me about many of their secrets for getting up for their morning moves. Here are just a few.

▸ The night before, lay your workout clothes and shoes next to your bed and get your workout area and ball ready so that you have no excuses when the alarm sounds.

▸ Write a note to yourself and place it in front of your alarm clock—something like "You can do it!" or "I deserve to feel fit."

▸ Say to yourself, "If I'm still this tired after two Daily Dozen moves, I can go back to bed."

▸ If you drink coffee, set your coffeemaker to start brewing 5 minutes before the alarm goes off. Let the smell of fresh coffee lure you from the covers.

▸ Go to bed earlier. You need a good night's sleep in order to wake up refreshed.

> "Feeling good about yourself involves more than a fit body. Commit yourself to constant self-improvement by challenging your mind as well as your body, and savor the feeling of self-accomplishment!"

day
2 THE DAILY DOZEN

UPPER-BACK STRETCH
(PAGE 116)

CHEST PRESS (PAGE 86)

TRADITIONAL CRUNCH
(PAGE 36)

FRONT RAISE (PAGE 96)

UPPER-BACK TONER
(PAGE 98)

BICEPS CURL (PAGE 108)

TRICEPS KICKBACK
(PAGE 104)

THIGH BLASTER (PAGE 58)

HAMSTRING STRETCH
(PAGE 126)

BALL SQUEEZE (PAGE 67)

BOTTOMS-UP (PAGE 66)

HAMSTRING CURL
(PAGE 64)

day
(2) YOUR EATING PLAN

	Calories	Carbohydrate	Protein	Fat
BREAKFAST				
Breakfast Burrito: Scramble 1 large egg and combine with 2 tablespoons salsa. Spoon into a 6" corn tortilla. **Orange wedges** **1 cup tea**	227	30.2 g	9.5 g	8.1 g
MIDMORNING 3 tablespoons popcorn (air-popped)	110	16 g	3 g	4 g
LUNCH				
Tuna Pita: Combine a 3-ounce can water-packed tuna and 2 tablespoons low-fat mayonnaise. Spoon into a 2-ounce whole wheat pita. **Radishes, sliced cucumber, and celery sticks** **1 pear**	494	66 g	28.2 g	15.3 g
MIDAFTERNOON 8 ounces vegetable juice 2 pieces light string cheese	170	12 g	15 g	6 g
DINNER				
Chicken and Vegetable Stir-Fry: Chop and sauté 1 boneless, skinless chicken breast (12 ounces raw weight) with garlic, grated gingerroot, and a small onion in 2 teaspoons olive oil for 2 to 3 minutes. Add 3 cups frozen Oriental vegetables, a dash of cayenne, and soy sauce to taste. Cook until the vegetables are crisp, about 5 minutes. (Use half for dinner and the rest for day 4's lunch.) **Cooked brown rice (¼ cup dry)**	498.8	42.2 g	53.6 g	12.9 g
TOTAL	**1,499.8**	**166.4 g** (44%)	**109.3 g** (29%)	**46.3 g** (28%)

{ I DID IT! } ▸

Name: Suzanne Dammeyer

Age: 35

Town: Annapolis, Maryland

Weight Lost: 40 pounds

Other Accomplishments: Wore a bikini for the first time in 11 years and climbed a mountain

before   after

"I got serious about weight loss after I turned 33 in April 2002. My dad had suffered a severe heart attack when he was 37. I weighed 180 pounds, my waist circumference was more than 34 inches, and my cholesterol levels were high. I knew I needed to take charge of my health or I would soon be following in my father's footsteps.

"I began keeping a food journal and working out to Denise's programs. I followed the 80/20 plan, making 80 percent of my diet very healthy and allowing myself little indulgences 20 percent of the time. I ate three meals a day, plus two or three snacks a day. I had lost and gained many times before, but I promised myself that this time I would lose the weight slowly and try to build muscle.

"Five months after starting, my coworkers noticed that I had lost weight (30 pounds by then). I went to Telluride, Colorado, and I was able to climb to the top of a nearby mountain. What a great feeling and a gorgeous view!

"I maintained my weight loss through the holidays, and in January committed myself to losing another 10 pounds. I lost the weight that spring and celebrated by going on a cruise and wearing a bikini for the first time in 11 years. My husband has also lost 25 pounds by following the same plan.

"I try to challenge myself by changing my workout routine. I work out 5 or 6 days a week, including weights three times a week, inline skating, Denise's tapes, yoga, walking, and the stability ball. I love to do this one exercise on the ball called the pike [a variation on the natural tummy tuck] by leaning on my hands like a pushup and raising my lower body up in a pike position. It's great for the abs. The stability ball is a great tool.

"Denise really does motivate me, and I want to thank her with all my heart for all this help."

Suzanne's Advice: Set small, achievable goals. Eat 80 percent healthy foods and 20 percent treats, using a food journal to keep yourself on track.

DENISE'S DAILY WISDOM

You may wonder why I've included a Daily Dozen routine for 6 out of 7 days a week. You may ask, "Don't I get more time off than that?" I have found that it takes time and repetition to form a habit. It's so easy to fall off the fitness wagon when you exercise only 3 days a week. If you feel tired on a particular day, you might say to yourself, "Oh, I'll exercise tomorrow." Eventually, you keep putting it off until another day that never comes. Make exercise a part of your life, just like brushing your teeth.

During this 3-week plan, you are forming many habits, but the most important one is the ability to find 12 minutes for *you* every day. If you've spent years catering to the needs of others and rarely ever giving yourself a second thought, finding 12 minutes every day to spend on just yourself will feel challenging at first. Move regularly and consistently, and you'll build a habit that will last a lifetime.

{ **"If you rest, you'll rust!"** }

day

3 THE DAILY DOZEN

HUG-A-BALL (PAGE 115)

SAW (PAGE 138)

**TRADITIONAL CRUNCH
(PAGE 36)**

OBLIQUE TWIST (PAGE 38)

TORSO TONER (PAGE 40)

MERMAID (PAGE 163)

BACK STRETCH (PAGE 35)

T-STAND (PAGE 140)

BACK TONER (PAGE 50)

**RECIPROCAL REACH
(PAGE 54)**

BICYCLE (PAGE 48)

**LOWER-TUMMY FIRMER
(PAGE 41)**

209

WEEK 1

day

(3) **YOUR EATING PLAN**

	Calories	Carbohydrate	Protein	Fat

BREAKFAST

Sweet and Crunchy Oatmeal:
Make plain oatmeal (1 packet or ½ cup dry) with 8 ounces fat-free milk. Stir in 2 tablespoons almonds, 2 tablespoons light syrup, 1 chopped medium apple, and a dash of cinnamon.

	Calories	Carbohydrate	Protein	Fat
	361	66 g	14.5 g	2.5 g

MIDMORNING
2 tangerines

	74	18.8 g	1 g	0.4 g

LUNCH

2 slices vegetable pizza (from a pizzeria; load on the veggies!)

	432	40 g	22 g	12 g

MIDAFTERNOON
½ cup hummus or other bean dip
2 ribs celery

	206	12.5 g	8.3 g	12 g

DINNER

Salmon with Salsa and Capers:
Sprinkle 1 piece of salmon (8 ounces raw weight) with a little Old Bay seasoning and broil or grill until cooked through, about 10 minutes. Combine ¼ cup salsa and a dash of hot-pepper sauce. Spoon on top of salmon and sprinkle with 1 tablespoon capers, drained.
1 cup steamed green beans
Quinoa (¼ cup dry), cooked in chicken broth with 1 tablespoon toasted onions

	499	27.9 g	54.9 g	17.1 g

	TOTAL	Calories	Carbohydrate	Protein	Fat
		1,572	**165.2 g** (42%)	**100.7 g** (26%)	**44 g** (25%)

{ I DID IT! } ▸

Name: Sheila Stillman

Age: 29

Town: Brunswick, New York

Weight Lost: 60 pounds

Other Accomplishments: Quit smoking, gained muscle strength, and dropped from a size 16 to a size 10

before   after

"During my teens and early twenties, I stayed active and involved in dancing, softball, bowling, and aerobics. At 5 feet 8 inches tall and with an athletic build, I weighed about 150 pounds. After graduating from college and meeting my future husband in 1995, however, I began to gain weight. In a few years, I gained about 60 pounds, topping out at 205. My friends called it my 'love weight.'

"My husband and I married in October 1997. I tried to lose some weight for the wedding but succeeded at shedding only 10 pounds. I started to exercise and walk the dog regularly but otherwise didn't change my lifestyle. I smoked, drank a lot of caffeine, and ate what I wanted, thinking I was being careful. During the next couple of years, I was diagnosed with an ear infection, then a eustachian tube disorder, and then heart palpitations. When my grandfather died of cancer in February 1999, I had an awakening.

"I began to pay more attention to what I ate. I read a study that found that women were more likely to succeed at quitting smoking and losing weight if they combined the goals rather than tried to meet them separately. With that, I jumped right in! I weaned myself off the smokes and began to exercise three times a week. I initially lost 10 pounds, but the weight loss seemed so slow. A friend at work who was a former bodybuilder suggested I keep a food diary. I began keeping my food diary, drinking a lot of water, limiting my sugars, taking vitamins, and eating a more balanced diet.

"By the spring of 2000, I had lost 60 pounds, weighing in at 145 pounds. Since then, I've added more weight training, and my weight has settled at 155 pounds. I feel more fit, toned, and slim than I have in years."

Sheila's Advice: Combine exercise with a well-balanced diet. Keep a food diary to help keep track of your calorie and fat consumption. Stay determined, and don't get discouraged.

day 4
(Wednesday)

Can you speed your results by tackling more than the Daily Dozen routines? The answer to that question depends on you. If it's a struggle for you to find 12 minutes a day to exercise, stick with only 12 minutes. Each Daily Dozen routine will certainly challenge your body and provide the results you seek. On the other hand, if you find that you move through your Daily Dozen routine easily and have time for more, then go for it. Here are some ways to optimize your results.

▸ Once you finish a Daily Dozen routine, do each exercise again for a total of two back-to-back routines.

▸ Do the day's suggested Daily Dozen routine in the morning and then again later in the day.

▸ Add cardio-on-the-ball moves to the Daily Dozen routine. You'll find these moves on pages 176 to 179.

{ "The joy lies in the journey, not in the destination. Enjoy each and every day. It's God's gift to us." }

day

(4) THE DAILY DOZEN

TRIANGLE (PAGE 160)

WARRIOR 2 (PAGE 158)

PUSHUP (PAGE 88)

LATERAL RAISE (PAGE 94)

ARM ROW (PAGE 92)

FRENCH CURL (PAGE 106)

CHEST STRETCH (PAGE 130)

HAMMER CURL (PAGE 110)

FRONT/BACK (PAGE 141)

BUTT AND THIGH FIRMER (PAGE 70)

QUAD SETS (PAGE 76)

FRONT-OF-THIGH STRETCH (PAGE 123)

day

4 YOUR EATING PLAN

	Calories	Carbohydrate	Protein	Fat
BREAKFAST				
Blueberry Smoothie: Blend 4 ounces fat-free milk, 4 ounces silken tofu, and 1 cup frozen or fresh blueberries. **1 whole grain roll with 2 teaspoons peanut butter**	360	38.5 g	24.6 g	13.4 g
MIDMORNING **8 ounces light yogurt**	100	16 g	6 g	0 g
LUNCH				
Stir-Fry Wrap: Heat leftover Chicken and Vegetable Stir-Fry from day 2. Serve in a whole wheat flour tortilla (6" diameter). **½ grapefruit**	352	35.1 g	29 g	10.9 g
MIDAFTERNOON **¼ cup roasted soybeans ("soy nuts")**	122	8 g	10 g	6 g
DINNER				
Italian Omelet: Whisk 2 large eggs, 2 extra egg whites, and 2 tablespoons fat-free milk. Pour egg mixture into pan, cook on medium heat until semiset, about 5 minutes. Add 1 cup frozen Italian-style vegetables, 1 tablespoon chopped sun-dried tomatoes, and 2 tablespoons Romano cheese, and fold one-half of the eggs over the vegetables. Cook until set. **Baked sweet potato (5" × 2")**	503.7	43.9 g	36.3 g	22.2 g
TOTAL	**1,437.7**	**141.5 g** (39%)	**105.9 g** (30%)	**52.5 g** (33%)

{ I DID IT! } ‣

Name: Peggy Birchfield

Age: 45

Town: Stafford, Vermont

Weight Lost: 21 pounds

Other Accomplishments: Shrank from a size 14 to a size 8

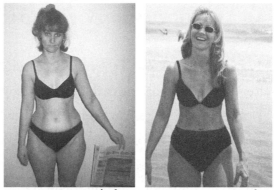

before   after

"I gained weight after I had children and never lost the extra pounds. Over a period of 10 years, not watching what I ate and not exercising began to add up. I went to the beach one day with a bunch of friends. Later, when I looked at photographs taken that day, I saw myself standing on the beach, and I freaked. I looked awful.

"I switched to a lower-fat, higher-protein diet, eliminated junk food, and began exercising regularly. My husband did the same, and we worked as a team. I now weigh 141 pounds and am still trying to get down to my goal of 138. Those last few pounds are the hardest. I feel so much better without the extra weight, and I have much more energy.

"I ride a stationary bike or walk on my treadmill each morning, and I work out with Denise in the evenings or in the morning three to four times a week. I have several of Denise's tapes and books that I consult for my workouts. I also read her Web site for diet tips.

"To stay motivated, I constantly read fitness magazines. I also keep motivational posters around my house to keep me going, and I try reading up on the latest forms of exercise. Variety and change keep exercise interesting. Denise also inspires me because she is close to my age. When I look at her, I think, 'I can look like that.' Her bubbly inspiration and strong faith have kept me working hard!"

Peggy's Advice: Persevere no matter what gets in your way. A healthy body is worth more than a million words. A friend can be one of the best boosters. Use Denise as your friend to keep going!

day 5
(Thursday)

DENISE'S DAILY WISDOM

My fans often ask me if they are "cheating" when they skip their cardio workouts after a long day working in the garden, moving furniture, or doing some other form of physical labor. I always reply, "No way!" Physical labor *is* a form of exercise. Weeding, digging holes, planting, lifting boxes, and moving furniture all require you to use your muscles. Think of 5 hours of gardening as a 5-hour-long workout. You're certainly not cheating if you skip an official exercise routine after that.

Cultivate the subtle art of listening to your body. Know the difference between when your body has *really* had enough and needs a rest and when your mind is merely trying to create excuses not to move.

{ "Respect and cherish your body.
You've been given only one. Taking care
of it is the key to a long, happy life." }

day
 5 THE DAILY DOZEN

1

**UPPER-BACK STRETCH
(PAGE 116)**

2
SIDE STRETCH (PAGE 118)

3
PILATES PLANK (PAGE 143)

4
**NATURAL TUMMY TUCK
(PAGE 46)**

5

RISE AND SHINE (PAGE 52)

6

**LOWER-BACK
STRENGTHENER (PAGE 51)**

7
BRIDGE (PAGE 165)

8

HIP CIRCLES (PAGE 142)

9

PELVIC TILT (PAGE 34)

10
**TUMMY FLATTENER
(PAGE 42)**

11

T-STAND (PAGE 140)

12

KNEE SWAY (PAGE 169)

217
WEEK 1

day

(5) **YOUR EATING PLAN**

	Calories	Carbohydrate	Protein	Fat

BREAKFAST
1 cup high-fiber cereal
8 ounces fat-free milk
2 tablespoons slivered almonds

Calories	Carbohydrate	Protein	Fat
329	50.5 g	15.4 g	9.9 g

MIDMORNING
1 medium Granny Smith apple

Calories	Carbohydrate	Protein	Fat
81	21.1 g	0.3 g	0.5 g

LUNCH
Spinach Salad:
  Combine 2 cups baby spinach, 4 slices
  turkey bacon, 1 chopped large hard-cooked
  egg, ½ cup drained water chestnuts. Toss
  with ¼ cup light raspberry vinaigrette.
**1 cup tomato soup (made with 1 cup fat-
free milk)**

Calories	Carbohydrate	Protein	Fat
518	56.6 g	24.4 g	25.4 g

MIDAFTERNOON
1 cup low-fat cottage cheese mixed with
onion soup mix
½ sliced cucumber and pepper strips for
dipping

Calories	Carbohydrate	Protein	Fat
188	13.2 g	29.7 g	3 g

DINNER
Spicy Turkey Burger:
  Season 1 ground turkey breast burger (½
  pound raw) with Worcestershire sauce and
  Italian seasoning. Broil 5 to 7 minutes per
  side. Make sure juices run clear, and to be
  on the safe side, use a meat thermometer.
  Top with 1 roasted red pepper, sliced red
  onion, and flavored mustard. Serve on a
  whole grain English muffin.
Asparagus Spears:
  Coat 10 spears with 1 teaspoon olive oil
  and grill or sauté until crisp-tender, 5 to 7
  minutes.

Calories	Carbohydrate	Protein	Fat
396	28 g	51.5 g	8.9 g

	Calories	Carbohydrate	Protein	Fat
TOTAL	**1,512**	**169.4 g** (45%)	**121.3 g** (32%)	**47.7 g** (28%)

{ I DID IT! } ▸

Name: Tera Feigen

Age: 39

Town: Watchung, New Jersey

Weight Lost: 30 pounds

Other Accomplishments: Shrank from a size 10 to a size 4

before   after

"Soon after turning 36, I experienced a classic midlife crisis and decided that it was time to make some changes in my life. At the top of my list was my weight, which was pushing 145 pounds. I wanted to be myself and to live my life to the fullest—and I knew I needed to lose weight in order to make those goals a reality.

"I lost 30 pounds by watching my diet and exercising to Denise's videos. Denise inspired me to keep going. She's a great role model for me, as she's about my age and still looks amazing. She communicates unconditional acceptance. That really kept me going.

"I am an overachiever by nature and place a lot of pressure on myself. I like doing workouts with Denise because she's such a real person, so gentle and loving and enthusiastic. Her messages are positive and uplifting, not pressuring. I have never felt bad about myself with Denise. *Au contraire*— I've always been inspired by her and felt fully supported by her!

"As with many people, I'm under stress and lead a busy life. Yet I've managed to maintain my weight loss by staying aware of my food intake, exercising regularly, drinking lots of water, and taking care of my emotional needs so that I don't try to fill them with food. I am finally living the life I have always wanted. I celebrate life and myself every day. I never want to go back."

Tera's Advice: Don't give up. Make a decision about who you want to be and what you want to look like. It's your life. Realize that when you overeat or exercise infrequently, you are making a decision about who you want to be and what you want to look like. *Love* yourself thin, and remember that, as Denise says, you are worth it!

◂ . . . .

DENISE'S DAILY WISDOM

Don't forget to celebrate your successes. Too often we only notice when we slip up. We spend the day thinking, "What's wrong with me that I slept in?" or "I didn't work hard enough on my Daily Dozen." You'll find more motivation, however, if you focus on each and every success.

Congratulate yourself for getting up earlier to fit in your routines. Be proud of your ability to perform a new Daily Dozen workout that you've never before attempted. Be constantly on the lookout for these little successes. They will serve as the kindling that fuels your desire to stay on track.

{ **"Laugh hard as often as possible.
It's the best natural medicine for the mind,
and it firms your tummy!"** }

day

6 THE DAILY DOZEN

MERMAID (PAGE 163)

CHEST PRESS (PAGE 86)

BACK AND SHOULDER
FIRMER (PAGE 99)

SHOULDER STRETCH
(PAGE 128)

ROWING SERIES (PAGE 150)

ARM FIRMER (PAGE 105)

ARM STRETCH (PAGE 131)

BICEPS CURL (PAGE 108)

BALL TAP (PAGE 62)

LOWER-BODY TONER
(PAGE 68)

LEG CIRCLES WITH BALL
(PAGE 147)

LAT PULLDOWN (PAGE 111)

day

(6) **YOUR EATING PLAN**

	Calories	Carbohydrate	Protein	Fat
BREAKFAST				
1 whole wheat English muffin 3 ounces smoked salmon Sliced onion 1 orange	255	40.3 g	12.4 g	2.6 g
MIDMORNING				
½ melon 8 ounces light yogurt	194	38.3 g	8.3 g	0.7 g
LUNCH				
Ham and Cheese Pita: Spread mustard inside a 2-ounce whole wheat pita and fill it with 3 ounces shaved ham, 1 slice Swiss cheese, sliced tomatoes, and lettuce.	316	35.7 g	25 g	9.9 g
MIDAFTERNOON				
¼ cup almonds	170	5 g	6 g	14 g
DINNER				
Flank Steak: Marinate a 1-pound flank steak in light red-wine vinaigrette for about 4 hours, then grill or broil it, 5 to 7 minutes per side. Cut into 4 slices, each 6" × 1" × ½" thick. (Use 2 for dinner and the other 2 for day 8's lunch.) **Garlic Potatoes:** Thinly slice 1 Idaho baking potato (about 4" × 2") and sauté in 1 teaspoon olive oil for 15 to 20 minutes, or until golden. Sprinkle with garlic powder. **2 cups steamed broccoli**	638	66 g	43.7 g	22.3 g
TOTAL	**1,573**	**185.3 g** (47%)	**95.4 g** (24%)	**49.5 g** (28%)

{ I DID IT! } ▸

Name: Mia Skaggs

Age: 38

Town: Hot Springs, Arkansas

Weight Lost: 28 pounds

Other Accomplishments: Lowered her cholesterol and firmed up her body

before   after

"Last year, my stomach started to bother me, so I went to my doctor. I was diagnosed with acid reflux. My doctor also told me that my cholesterol count was 347, which is 147 points above normal. I was stunned. To help bring my cholesterol under control, my doctor prescribed diet and exercise.

"When my sister learned of my diagnosis, she sent me a Denise Austin video, and I began working out 5 or 6 days a week with Denise. I cut my fat intake as well, and the weight began to fall off of me. After 4 months, I dropped from 146 pounds to 126 pounds and lowered my cholesterol to 224.

"I visited the doctor again after 8 months, when my weight had dropped all the way down to 118. The doctors and nurses at the office were all impressed, and I felt so happy and proud of myself. My cholesterol has since risen some, so I now take a prescription medication to lower it. I am still following my low-fat diet, and my weight has remained steady at 118.

"I love working out in the morning with Denise. I now have several of her videos from which to choose, many of which use the ball and band. I feel so much better. I feel energized and perky, kind of like the Energizer Bunny. My muscles have started firming up, and I think my arms look amazing!"

Mia's Advice: Get up and work out first thing in the morning. It takes such a short time to complete your routine, and you will benefit from it all day long. After a morning workout, you'll feel energized and ready to face the day.

DENISE'S DAILY WISDOM

Often, as people lose weight, they forget to shed their old images. Many people have told me that they walked around in their old size 16s for weeks before going out and buying size 12s or size 10s. Noticing your weight on the scale is important, but you'll gain a true sense of motivation when you notice the loose waistband on your pants!

As the weeks go on, don't be afraid to reach into the back of your closet and pull out those old clothes—the ones from your slimmer days. Try them on and relish the sensation of how they fit. And when these clothes become too roomy, treat yourself to a shopping spree and buy new, smaller outfits that show off your new body. This not only rewards you for your efforts, it is also a subtle way of committing to keep the weight off. If you walk around in your old baggy clothes, your inner voice will whisper, "Why spend money on new clothes? I might gain it back." Once you spend money on new, smaller clothes, you'll find renewed motivation to keep the pounds off. Let your clothing be the barometer of your success. As soon as it starts to feel snug, you'll know you need to step up the effort. You are worth it!

> "We all need to feel appreciated. Tell someone you love how much you treasure him or her. A smile, a compliment, one kind sentence—those little things can make a person's day."

day

⑦ THE DAILY DOZEN

UPPER-BACK STRETCH
(PAGE 116)

WAIST ROTATION/LOWER-
BACK STRETCH (PAGE 117)

SIDE STRETCH (PAGE 118)

THIGH STRETCH (PAGE 119)

SPINAL TWIST (PAGE 121)

TORSO STRETCH (PAGE 122)

FRONT-OF-THIGH STRETCH
(PAGE 123)

HIP RELEASE (PAGE 124)

CHEST STRETCH (PAGE 130)

SHOULDER STRETCH
(PAGE 128)

MERMAID (PAGE 163)

CHILD'S POSE (PAGE 132)

day

YOUR EATING PLAN

	Calories	Carbohydrate	Protein	Fat
BREAKFAST 1 cup high-fiber cereal 8 ounces fat-free milk 1 cup fresh or frozen mixed berries	286	50 g	16 g	4.3 g
MIDMORNING 1 kiwifruit	46	11.3 g	0.8 g	0.3 g
LUNCH 10¾-ounce can vegetable soup with ¼ cup dry barley added **Mushroom Omelet:** Beat 1 egg, 2 egg whites, Italian seasoning, sea salt, and black pepper. Sauté ½ cup mushrooms and 1 tablespoon chopped green onion in 1 tablespoon whipped butter. Add eggs and cook until set.	432	49.7 g	22.6 g	17.3 g
MIDAFTERNOON 2 ribs celery 2 tablespoons peanut butter	202	10 g	7.6 g	17.2 g
DINNER **Chicken Parmesan:** Pour ½ cup spaghetti sauce on top of 1 skinless chicken breast (6 ounces raw weight). Add a splash of hot-pepper sauce and 2 tablespoons Parmesan cheese. Bake at 350°F for about 30 minutes. **Bow-Tie Pasta and Asparagus:** Toss 1 cup cooked whole wheat bow-tie pasta with 1 teaspoon olive oil and garlic powder to taste. Mix with 1 cup asparagus pieces.	562.5	57.2 g	56.8 g	12 g
TOTAL	**1,528.5**	**178.2 g** (47%)	**103.8 g** (27%)	**51.1 g** (30%)

{ I DID IT! } ▸

Name: Laura Durava

Age: 41

Town: Mt. Prospect, Illinois

Weight Lost: 28 pounds

Other Accomplishments: Has maintained her weight loss for 8 years

before   after

"In 1995, before I got pregnant with my second child, I weighed 143 pounds. That's a lot for someone who's only 5 feet 2 inches tall. After having my baby, I decided to do something about it and get back in shape. I bought my first Denise Austin video in 1996, and I have been a loyal fan ever since.

"It took me 7 months of consistent exercise to lose the weight. I've since had a third child, but I quickly lost my baby weight. My weight has wavered between 113 and 120 pounds, but I have never come close to the weight I once was!

"In addition to doing Pilates and fat-burning workouts with Denise, I also use her step and re-sistance bands. I work out with her at least 4 days per week, for no more than 45 to 50 minutes a session.

"I keep a diary of my workouts and food intake to help me stay on track. I aim for 25 workouts per month, and once a week I let myself cheat on desserts or higher-calorie meals so that I don't feel deprived. One piece of equipment that has also encouraged me is the pedometer, which I bought a year ago. I aim for 10,000 steps a day, 6 days a week (in addition to my workouts). Some-times when I feel like snacking, I take a look at my pedometer, and if I'm not quite at my goal, I'll take a quick walk instead. It's a great way to keep on track.

"I know Denise hears all kinds of success stories, and it is so easy to see why she is loved around the world. She has changed my life, as I have more energy and stamina than ever before!"

Laura's Advice: Never go on a diet. "Dieting, to me, spells deprivation, wreaks havoc on your metabolism (putting it in the 'starvation' mode), and can lead to binges," she says. "I try to eat five small meals a day that total 2,000 calories. This may seem to be a tremendous amount, but it keeps my energy and sugar levels in check."

WEEK 2

Congratulations on completing week 1 of the 3-week plan! You are already one-third of the way toward your goal. Give yourself a pat on the back for a job well done. If you stuck with the program each day last week, that in itself is a significant accomplishment, one that you should be proud of. You are in the process of forming an incredibly important habit, in many ways the healthiest habit of all, exercising and eating right.

Despite your success, do you still find your thoughts focused on the negative? Do you find yourself brooding and feeling guilty about every single slipup? I encourage you to put aside your inner critic and let your inner confidence bloom. Each day start with a fresh slate, focusing on the new, fit, firm, healthy you that is blossoming. Think of yourself as a rose early in its season, closed tightly. Slowly and over time the petals begin to unfold, revealing the beauty inside.

In the coming week, your toning routines will become slightly more difficult. If you encounter an exercise that feels too challenging, move back to the less-challenging version of the exercise. For example, on day 9, I suggest that you complete intermediate biceps curls. It's a tough one! If you can't balance on the ball with one leg extended and simultaneously do the biceps curls, feel free to go back to the beginner version. Don't beat yourself up or feel discouraged. Your balance and strength will improve over time.

If you want to lose more than 5 pounds, step up your cardio this week from 12 to 24 minutes, three to four times a week. You can do your cardio on any day you like, as long as you *do it*.

Continue to monitor your water intake and your hours of sleep, always aiming for more. Until you form a habit, which takes 3 weeks, it can be easy to backslide.

You'll start your week with your day off from exercise, your weigh-in, and your preparation for the week to come. I believe your "day off" can actually be the most productive and crucial day of the week; it's the day that you take care of all the details that will help you accomplish your goals for the week to come.

This week, don't forget to focus on *quality* in everything you choose for yourself—not only in your food and fitness but also in the way you think about your downtime. Are you giving yourself enough true rest? Are you taking as good care of *you* as you are of those you love? Savor the feeling of a good, deep stretch and try to transfer that pleasure to other parts of your life—you're worth it!

day 8
(Sunday)

DENISE'S DAILY WISDOM

I like to make fitness as fun as possible. The more fun you have, the more likely you'll stick with it. Each weekend, I like to organize a fun family day, on which my husband and girls do something active together. Although I often don't think of it as "official" exercise, it is. Each Sunday, I recommend that you do the same. You will find that as you grow stronger and more coordinated, you'll want to do more and more. Spend the day at the park, swimming in the pool, playing tag and other active games with your children, hiking on a nature trail, going on a bike ride, gardening in your yard, or just dancing in your living room. The more you move, the more calories you'll burn—even if it doesn't feel like exercise. It's all about being more active. Just move, move, move.

{ "What we are is God's gift to us. What we become is our gift to God." }

day
8 THE DAILY DOZEN

Day Off!

Today is your day off from exercise. Spend the day appreciating your accomplishments for the past week. Remember to stay on track, find a *fun* type of exercise today, but don't add up how many calories you've burned. Just have fun in your body as it gets more fit each day.

Weigh-In

Assess your progress. Don't worry if you don't see dramatic changes in your weight or measurements—your body is keeping track, even if the scale isn't yet. Record:

- Your current weight
- Your current measurements
- Your "yea, me!" moments (any other accomplishments, such as baggy clothing or more energy to run up stairs)

Reflection

As in week 1, a few thoughts will get you mentally prepared for the days ahead.

1. What did you do well last week?

2. How could you improve your motivation and dedication?

3. Set one goal that you plan to accomplish in the coming week. (For example, plan to get up 5 minutes earlier, give up eating past 7:00 P.M., and so forth.)

Preparation

On page 295, you'll find a shopping list of items that you will need for the next week's menus and recipes. Shop for those items today. Then, complete any preparatory tasks that will help make the rest of your week go more smoothly. For example, you could chop some vegetables to get them ready ahead of time.

day

8 YOUR EATING PLAN

	Calories	Carbohydrate	Protein	Fat

BREAKFAST
½ melon
1 cup low-fat cottage cheese
1 slice whole grain toast with fruit spread
1 cup tea

| | 321 | 40.4 g | 32.4 g | 4.9 g |

MIDMORNING
1 (1½-ounce) pear

| | 98 | 25.1 g | 0.7 g | 0.7 g |

LUNCH
Flank Steak Fajita:
Heat 2 slices of flank steak (from day 6's dinner) with sautéed onions and peppers. Sauté onions and peppers in 1 teaspoon olive oil for about 5 minutes. Spoon the mixture and some salsa into a whole wheat or corn tortilla.
1 tangerine

| | 522 | 39.7 g | 35.2 g | 20.2 g |

MIDAFTERNOON
¼ cup roasted soybeans

| | 122 | 8 g | 10 g | 6 g |

DINNER
Turkey and Mixed Greens Salad:
Toss 2 cups mixed greens with ½ cucumber, 1 tomato, ½ pepper, and orange sections. Add 4 ounces deli peppered turkey breast. Sprinkle on 2 tablespoons Parmesan cheese. Drizzle with 2 tablespoons raspberry vinaigrette.
1 (2" to 2½") whole grain roll

| | 464 | 61.8 g | 34.6 g | 10.3 g |

| TOTAL | 1,527 | 175 g (46%) | 112.9 g (30%) | 42.1 g (25%) |

{I DID IT!} ▸

Name: Dayne O. Zinser

Age: 40

Town: Columbus, Ohio

Weight Lost: 60 pounds

Other Accomplishments: Went from a
40-inch waist to a 32-inch waist

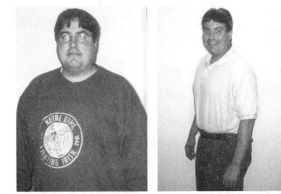

before   after

"Every time I tell my weight-loss story, my son, Destin, says, 'Dad, I'm tired of hearing this.' I still tell everyone I see, because I'm so proud of what I have accomplished.

"My story begins in April 2001. One weekend, my son walked into the kitchen and said out of the blue, 'Dad, I think you need to start eating at Subway.' He had seen the commercials about how Jared had lost weight by eating only at Subway, and he thought I could do the same. There's nothing like getting hit between the eyes with a two-by-four. He opened my eyes to my weight problem.

"To lose the weight, I began walking 2½ miles every day. One morning, I got up and exercised with Denise. I was hooked. After that, I bought one of her videos. I soon got into the routine of walking 2½ miles and then coming home and popping in her video. What a workout! It was hard at first, but the weight just melted off. Denise always says, 'You're burning butter,' and she's right. That first year, I lost 50 pounds.

"My sister helped me lose the last 10 by teaching me to read nutrition labels and check the number of fat grams in the food I ate. Now I read every label for the food I purchase. I even have taught my son to read labels. I never did go to Subway to lose the weight. Instead, I made smarter eating choices. For example, I switched from regular bread to light bread, from fatty snacks to fat-free pretzels, and from red meat to a salad with grilled chicken breast cooked on my George Foreman grill.

"Fitness and nutrition are now the top priorities in my life. My goal is to motivate my son to follow in my footsteps."

Dayne's Advice: Put your fat photo on your refrigerator and in your car. "Every time I think about raiding the fridge, I look at the picture and realize that I never want to look like that again," he says. He also suggests brushing your teeth when you get the urge to eat something late at night. "It takes your mind off food and cleans your teeth at the same time," he adds.

· · · · · · · ▶

DENISE'S DAILY WISDOM

You can help yourself stick to reasonable food portions by starting the day on the right foot nutritionally. Research shows that eating and drinking sugary foods such as doughnuts, baked goods, and soft drinks often result in hunger and cravings later in the day. I recommend that you make breakfast your opportunity to eat some great foods with fiber, fruits, vegetables, and protein.

Try a bowl of oatmeal with a spoonful of ground flaxseeds and some berries. Or have an egg-white omelet chock-full of veggies. One of my favorite breakfast options is a bowl of high-fiber cereal with fat-free milk and berries. Such meals have staying power, helping to prevent cravings and hunger all morning. They will stabilize your blood sugar and help you to eat right for the rest of the day.

{ "Prevention is the best medicine.
Never take your health for granted." }

UPPER-BACK STRETCH (PAGE 116)

PUSHUP (PAGE 88)

INTERMEDIATE FRONT RAISE (PAGE 97)

BUG (PAGE 139)

BACK AND SHOULDER FIRMER (PAGE 99)

INTERMEDIATE BICEPS CURL (PAGE 109)

TRICEPS KICKBACK (PAGE 104)

INTERMEDIATE THIGH BLASTER (PAGE 59)

HIP STRETCH (PAGE 125)

ADVANCED BALL SQUEEZE (PAGE 67)

BOTTOMS-UP (PAGE 66)

INTERMEDIATE HAMSTRING CURL (PAGE 65)

day

(9) YOUR EATING PLAN

	Calories	Carbohydrate	Protein	Fat

BREAKFAST
Strawberry Smoothie:
Blend 8 ounces light fruit-flavored yogurt, 4 ounces fat-free milk, ½ cup frozen strawberries, and ¼ cup almonds.

| | 336 | 33.5 g | 16.3 g | 14.4 g |

MIDMORNING
2 pieces light string cheese

| | 120 | 0 g | 14 g | 6 g |

LUNCH
Salmon Pita:
Take a 2-ounce whole wheat pita and fill it with 3 ounces smoked salmon, lettuce, tomato, and 1 tablespoon capers.
1 apple

| | 327 | 56.8 g | 23.3 g | 3.4 g |

MIDAFTERNOON
½ cup hummus
1 cup raw broccoli and ½ cup grape tomatoes for dipping

| | 170 | 27.2 g | 7 g | 9 g |

DINNER
Chili:
Brown 1 pound extra-lean sirloin in ¼ cup water and add 1 chopped onion. Cook until meat is brown. Add a 26-ounce can flavored, diced tomatoes; 14½-ounce can kidney beans (drained); and chili powder to taste and heat through. (For dinner, eat 1½ cups of chili; save the rest for lunch tomorrow.)
1 handful baked tortilla chips
Orange wedges

| | 612 | 74.1 g | 48 g | 13.2 g |

| **TOTAL** | **1,565** | **191.6 g** (49%) | **108.6 g** (28%) | **46 g** (26%) |

{ I DID IT! } ▸

Name: Cassie Major

Age: 38

Town: Miamisburg, Ohio

Weight Lost: 42 pounds

Other Accomplishments: Shrank from a size 16 to a size 8, lost 3 inches from her hips

before   after

"Most of my adult life, I've worn a clothing size of a 9 or 10. Then came nursing school, stress, and child number two. My grandmother always said that she never knew anyone who loved food as much as I do. I turned to food to calm my stress, and my weight went up from there.

"As I crept closer to a size 18, I felt fat from the inside out. I didn't like how I looked or felt. Denise helped me turn things around. I saw Denise on the *Donny and Marie* talk show, just before their show was canceled. As I listened to Denise talk, I felt more and more determined to do something about my weight. I went to the grocery store, stocked up on healthful foods, and began watching my portions and exercising.

"Obsession kicked in, and even when my husband and I took our kids on vacation to Sea-World, I packed healthful foods to eat during vacation and kept them all in a cooler. I began to feel as if I could control my food intake. It took me 9 months to lose the weight.

"Today, I am 42 pounds lighter and have never been in better shape or felt better. For the past 3 years, I have been working out three to five times a week and love it. I actually get quite cranky if I miss a day. I feel really good after I work out, which creates a chain reaction that helps me to eat well for the rest of the day. I still love food, but I have learned to focus on foods that are good for me. I snack, but I do it in moderation. I occasionally have a treat, but I tend to split things with the kids or my husband so I don't overindulge.

"I feel so much better when I shop for clothing. I can pick out clothes that, in the past, I couldn't wear. When I fit into my size 8s comfortably, or at times in a size 6, that makes my day."

Cassie's Advice: Getting fit allows you to participate in life to the fullest. You will feel 500 percent better and more inclined to be active with your family. You will be able to play sports with your children, whose friends will think you are "way cool" for doing so.

day 10
(Tuesday)

. . . . ▸ **DENISE'S DAILY WISDOM**

Many of my fans ask me how to get over those motivational slumps. They tell me that they find it easy to motivate themselves for a while, and then they enter a period of time when they hate to exercise and don't know what to do about it.

Is this true for you, too? Here are some ways to get over the hump that have worked for me and other people I've spoken with.

▸ Exercise with your honey or a friend. You'll feel accountable to that person. By setting up a time and a place, you will have to keep your promise.

▸ Mix it up. Doing the same thing day in and day out becomes boring. That's why I've provided so much variety in the ball and band routines in this book.

▸ Pump up the volume. Your favorite music can help create the urge to move.

▸ Stick with it. Usually, motivational slumps pass by, and eventually your motivation resurfaces. Persevere, and eventually you won't even recognize the person who wanted to skip those workouts.

{ "Oxygen creates energy. Breathe deeply and nourish your body with this important life force. One of the best ways to get more oxygen flowing is by exercising. Exercise equals energy!" }

day

10 THE DAILY DOZEN

WAIST ROTATION/LOWER-BACK STRETCH (PAGE 117)

PILATES TWIST (PAGE 137)

HIP RELEASE (PAGE 124)

INTERMEDIATE CRUNCH (PAGE 37)

ADVANCED OBLIQUE TWIST (PAGE 39)

INTERMEDIATE TORSO TONER (PAGE 40)

BACK STRETCH (PAGE 35)

T-STAND (PAGE 140)

INTERMEDIATE RISE AND SHINE (PAGE 52)

RECIPROCAL REACH (PAGE 54)

WAISTLINE TRIMMER (PAGE 43)

ROLL-DOWN (PAGE 144)

day

(10) YOUR EATING PLAN

	Calories	Carbohydrate	Protein	Fat

BREAKFAST

1 ½ cups toasted oats cereal
8 ounces fat-free milk
½ grapefruit

Calories	Carbohydrate	Protein	Fat
291	62.2 g	13.1 g	3 g

MIDMORNING

1 kiwifruit

Calories	Carbohydrate	Protein	Fat
46	11.3 g	0.8 g	0.3 g

LUNCH

1 cup Chili (from last night's dinner)
2 cups mixed greens
2 tablespoons light dressing
1 handful baked tortilla chips

Calories	Carbohydrate	Protein	Fat
461	46.7 g	31.7 g	14.2 g

MIDAFTERNOON

2 hard-cooked eggs
8 ounces vegetable juice

Calories	Carbohydrate	Protein	Fat
198	12.2 g	13.4 g	10 g

DINNER

Tuna and Vegetable Teriyaki Kebabs:
Marinate 8 ounces tuna in teriyaki sauce,
cut it into cubes, and place it on skewers
with chunks of zucchini (1 small),
mushrooms (½ cup), and onion
(1 medium). Grill for 7 to 10 minutes.

Baked Sweet Potato:
Bake 2 sweet potatoes, each about
5" long, at 350°F for 45 to 60 minutes,
or until cooked through. Sprinkle with
cinnamon. (Eat one now and save the
other for lunch tomorrow.)

Calories	Carbohydrate	Protein	Fat
540	45.6 g	57.6 g	12.5 g

	Calories	Carbohydrate	Protein	Fat
TOTAL	**1,536**	**178 g** (46%)	**116.6 g** (30%)	**40 g** (23%)

{ I DID IT! } ▸

Name: Stephanie Piecuch

Age: 35

Town: Mayfield Village, Ohio

Weight Lost: 62 pounds

Other Accomplishments: Boosted her energy level and confidence

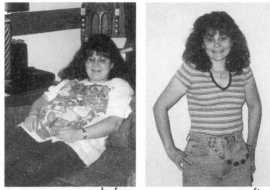

before   after

"I gained weight through my pregnancies. With my first baby, I went way overboard and gained 67 pounds! My husband bought me one of Denise's books, and I followed her advice religiously. I lost all but 5 pounds. During my subsequent two pregnancies, I did a little better and gained just 50 or so pounds and then lost that weight after my deliveries.

"My eating habits during those pregnancies were still not stellar, but I managed to stay in shape by exercising to pregnancy videos. My labor and delivery for those two births went a lot easier, and I attribute it to being in top shape. I know I would have gained a lot more weight if I had not been working out.

"I am now in a size 8. I still exercise with Denise. I do aerobics three times a week and use her *Hit the Spot!* tapes twice a week. My biggest challenge still is eating. I love food. I found lots of recipes in Denise's books and on her Web site, and they helped me to stay on track. Her recipes are so simple and quick, and they taste great.

"I would not be in as good health and shape if it were not for Denise and my husband (who bought me her book). I am now happy, have three kids, and every day I hear people tell me that I still look great."

Stephanie's Advice: If you are planning to have a baby, Stephanie suggests that you first get in shape. "Lose the weight *before* you get pregnant," she says. "Once you're pregnant, if your doctor okays it, exercise to a workout tape designed for pregnant women."

DENISE'S DAILY WISDOM

Some people try to speed up their results by exercising their trouble spots every day. For example, they do a leg workout every day or an abs workout every day. Rather than speed results, however, this might be a recipe for injury. Your muscles need a day to recover from resistance exercise. If you work the same muscle group every single day, it never gets a chance to recover and grow stronger. Worse, you feel sore and tired all of the time, which depletes your motivational reserves.

You'll notice that my 3-week plan never includes strengthening exercises of the same body area 2 days in a row. This allows each body area to completely recover. Successful weight loss requires patience. Stick with the 3-week plan as it is laid out, and hold yourself back from adding to it. Your results will come. I promise.

{ "Nothing <u>tastes</u> as good
as feeling good feels!" }

INTERMEDIATE TRIANGLE
(PAGE 161)

INTERMEDIATE WARRIOR 2
(PAGE 159)

ADVANCED CHEST PRESS
(PAGE 87)

**INTERMEDIATE LATERAL
RAISE (PAGE 95)**

UPRIGHT ROW (PAGE 100)

**INTERMEDIATE FRENCH
CURL (PAGE 107)**

**INTERMEDIATE BICEPS
CURL (PAGE 109)**

WALL SQUAT (PAGE 60)

FLOOR TAP (PAGE 63)

**ULTIMATE TUMMY
TRIMMER (PAGE 47)**

HIP CIRCLES (PAGE 142)

OUTER-THIGH TONER
(PAGE 69)

day

(11) YOUR EATING PLAN

	Calories	Carbohydrate	Protein	Fat

BREAKFAST

Ham and Cheddar Breakfast Sandwich:
Split 1 whole wheat English muffin. Insert
2 slices baked ham (deli slices) and ¼ cup
shredded light Cheddar. Heat until the
cheese melts.
½ cantaloupe

	324	48.3 g	23.3 g	7.7 g

MIDMORNING
1 tangerine

	37	9.4 g	1 g	0.2 g

LUNCH

Shrimp and Spinach Salad:
Toss 2 cups spinach with 1 cup frozen
baby shrimp, ½ cup drained water chestnuts, 2 slices turkey bacon, ¼ cup drained
chickpeas, and 2 tablespoons light dressing.
**Baked sweet potato (from yesterday's
dinner)**
6-ounce can vegetable juice

	501.5	61.4 g	32.1 g	13 g

MIDAFTERNOON
¼ cup almonds

	170	5 g	6 g	14 g

DINNER

Stuffed Shells:
Put 6 prepared cheese-stuffed shells in
baking pan. Cover with a bottled spaghetti
sauce and add a little fresh basil and
balsamic vinegar. Cook at 350°F for 30
minutes. (*Note*: Requires 2 minutes of
prep, but 30 minutes of baking time. Eat 3
shells for dinner and save the other 3 for
day 13's lunch.)
**1 cup steamed green beans with ½ cup
canned or fresh mushrooms**

	444	72.8 g	30.4 g	10.4 g

TOTAL	1,476.5	196.9 g (53%)	92.8 g (25%)	45.3 g (28%)

{ I DID IT! } ▸

Name: Julie Graver

Age: 35

Town: Marysville, Washington

Weight Lost: 32 pounds

Other Accomplishments: Went from a size 6 to a size 0 and gained 5 pounds of muscle

before   after

"When I got married at age 24, I began taking birth control pills and gained 35 pounds over the next 4 years. I am only 5 feet 1 inch tall and have a very small frame, so I really could not carry the weight! I bought Denise's *Fat-Burning Blast* video and used that tape regularly for 10 months. The weight came off, and I dropped from a high of 124 pounds back down to a low of 92 pounds and from a size 6 to a size 0. I then concentrated on strength training and gained 5 pounds of muscle—and I still wear a size 0.

"Over the years, I have enjoyed working out with Denise. I rotate my exercises all the time to keep my workouts fresh. I enjoy using the stability ball, as it helps improve balance and strengthen my lower back. In fact, I recently injured my back, and many of the exercises the physical therapist showed me were the ones that Denise suggests! My physical therapist was very impressed. I also really like pairing a resistance band with Pilates postures. The resistance band really challenges me, strengthens my core, and improves my flexibility.

"Denise has really helped keep me motivated with her positive attitude. I only work out at home, which can be hard to have the discipline to do, but Denise is my own personal cheerleader! I am proud of myself when I'm done with my workout."

Julie's Advice: "Have fun and laugh at yourself. Don't weigh yourself; instead, measure your progress by how your clothes fit. Try eating six times a day to keep cravings under control. And finally, be proud of yourself for accomplishing a workout and smile before, during, and after working out. The smile will lift your spirit and the spirits of those around you."

day 12
(Thursday)

. . . . ▶

DENISE'S DAILY WISDOM

You can more effectively keep track of your eating habits and rein in what I like to call "unconscious calories" by keeping a food diary. Each day, jot down everything that you eat. Include little nibbles here and there—the bites you finished from your child's plate, the free samples you had at the grocery store, the taste of cake you indulged in at an office party. At the end of the day, look over your food diary. Notice not only how much and how often you ate but also the composition of your meals. Are you eating enough fruits and vegetables? Your food diary will help you to find out. Are you eating too many sweets or drinking too many soft drinks? The answers will be right there in front of you at the end of that day.

One caution, however: Don't allow your food diary to make you feel guilty. Just use it as a way to keep tabs on your eating habits. In fact, I recommend that you toss out each diary entry after you have looked it over. This allows you to start over the next day with a fresh slate and without guilt.

{ "Why are you working so hard?
For your health, for your body,
for your mind, for you—that's why!" }

1

UPPER-BACK STRETCH
(PAGE 116)

2

WAIST ROTATION/LOWER-
BACK STRETCH (PAGE 117)

3

PLANK (PAGE 44)

4

COBRA (PAGE 164)

5

LOWER-BACK
STRENGTHENER (PAGE 51)

6

INTERMEDIATE TORSO
TONER (PAGE 40)

7

BACK STRETCH (PAGE 35)

8

OBLIQUE TWIST (PAGE 38)

9

DOUBLE-LEG STRETCH
(PAGE 148)

10

WAISTLINE TRIMMER
(PAGE 43)

11

INTERMEDIATE BICYCLE
(PAGE 49)

12

KNEE SWAY (PAGE 169)

day

(12) **YOUR EATING PLAN**

	Calories	Carbohydrate	Protein	Fat
BREAKFAST				
Smoked Salmon and Egg Pita: Fill a 2-ounce whole wheat pita with 1 scrambled egg and 1 slice smoked salmon. ½ cantaloupe	358	51.9 g	25.5 g	7.7 g
MIDMORNING 8 ounces light yogurt	100	16 g	6 g	0 g
LUNCH 1 spinach and cheese calzone (from a pizzeria)	440	46 g	21 g	19 g
MIDAFTERNOON ¾ cup low-fat cottage cheese mixed with ½ packet onion soup mix 4 ribs celery for dipping	144	8.3 g	21.8 g	2.2 g
DINNER **Shrimp Stir-Fry:** Sauté ½ bag frozen baby shrimp (5 ounces) in 1 teaspoon olive oil with garlic, grated gingerroot, and a dash of cayenne until shrimp turn pink, about 5 minutes. Add 2 cups of frozen Oriental vegetables, 1 ounce peanuts, and ½ cup water chestnuts. Add soy sauce to taste. Cook for another 5 minutes, or until vegetables are crisp-tender. **Cooked brown rice (¼ cup dry)**	477	57.5 g	38.6 g	18.6 g
TOTAL	**1,519**	**179.7 g** (47%)	**112.9 g** (30%)	**47.5 g** (28%)

{ I DID IT! } ▸

Name: Lori Edwards

Age: 60

Town: York, Pennsylvania

Weight Lost: 50 pounds

Other Accomplishments: Went from a size 18 to a size 6 and reduced stress

before   after

"My struggle with weight management is as old as I am. I was chubby as a child, and I learned to eat for every occasion and to soothe every emotion. During my teen years, I trimmed down to a svelte size 5 but then later gained back the weight during my second and third pregnancies. I lost weight after each pregnancy by counting calories and exercising.

"During the 1970s, I suffered a herniated disk in my back after being thrown off a horse. I was unable to walk and function for more than a year, and I gained a lot of weight, topping out at 180 pounds. I tried countless diets, but I couldn't lose a pound!

"I told myself the usual stuff, that it was my metabolism, that it was the fault of my genetics. Finally, in February 2001, I vacationed at Virginia Beach with my daughter Rebecca. She did all of the cooking and allowed me to eat only what she prepared. Each day we walked 10 to 24 blocks on the beach, and at night we worked out to wonderful Denise Austin tapes. I felt fantastic. I lost 17 pounds in 6 weeks.

"I continued on this program after I returned home, writing down my meals and exercising with Denise. By September of that year, I had lost all 50 pounds. I am now 60 years young! People can't believe my age. I look better now than I did at age 30, 40, and 50. I feel better, too. I now have Denise's stability ball, which I love. I've gone from a size 18 to a size 6. I even have a waistline."

Lori's Advice: Keep a photo on your fridge that reminds you of your goal every time you open the refrigerator door. "When I look at the fat photo of me on my fridge, I am reminded that there is an ember still inside of me, which, without perseverance, can fuel into a fire of fat," she says.

day 13
(Friday)

DENISE'S DAILY WISDOM

I try not to eat any food that contains partially hydrogenated fat. Also called trans fat, this type of fat has been implicated in heart disease, cancer, and weight gain. The worst offenders include margarine, cake and other mixes, instant soups, fast food, frozen dinners and desserts, commercially baked goods, snack chips and crackers, breakfast cereals, and commercially made dips and salad dressings. Trans fats are found mainly in packaged foods.

During the late 1970s, before the dangers of these fats were known, food manufacturers began using partially hydrogenated oils to extend the shelf life of packaged foods. For many years, trans fat was considered a hidden fat because manufacturers were not required to list it on food labels. Fortunately, so much evidence is now stacked against these fats that the FDA now requires manufacturers to list them on labels.

Examine the labels of the packaged foods you eat for their levels of trans fats. If possible, buy only packaged foods that contain zero trans fat.

{ "Attitude is everything, so pick a good one!" }

day
(13) **THE DAILY DOZEN**

MERMAID (PAGE 163)

**ADVANCED PUSHUP
(PAGE 89)**

CHEST FIRMER (PAGE 90)

**INTERMEDIATE ARM ROW
(PAGE 92)**

FLOOR TAP (PAGE 63)

**BACK AND SHOULDER
FIRMER (PAGE 99)**

**SHOULDER STRETCH
(PAGE 128)**

ROWING SERIES (PAGE 150)

ARM STRETCH (PAGE 131)

BICEPS CURL (PAGE 108)

THIGH SHAPER (PAGE 78)

CHILD'S POSE (PAGE 132)

day

(13) **YOUR EATING PLAN**

	Calories	Carbohydrate	Protein	Fat

BREAKFAST

Spiced Oatmeal:
Make oatmeal (1 packet or ½ cup dry) with 4 ounces fat-free milk. Stir in 2 tablespoons light syrup and 1 finely chopped McIntosh apple. Sprinkle with allspice, cinnamon, or nutmeg.

| 351 | 57.1 g | 9.8 g | 3.3 g |

MIDMORNING
½ cup roasted soybeans

| 245 | 16.5 g | 20 g | 13 g |

LUNCH

3 Stuffed Shells (from day 11's dinner)
Fresh Veggie Salad:
Toss 1 cup vegetables (grape tomatoes, mushrooms, zucchini, onion, broccoli) with 2 tablespoons light vinaigrette, and add 1 chopped shallot and fresh chopped basil.

| 461 | 65.7 g | 27.1 g | 15.5 g |

MIDAFTERNOON
½ mango

| 67 | 17.6 g | 0.5 g | 0.3 g |

DINNER

Stuffed Chicken Breast:
Thinly cut chicken tenderloins (1 package; ½ pound raw weight is the serving size). Mix up 1 cup prepared stuffing and add fresh parsley and 1 tablespoon chopped onion. Divide evenly among the chicken pieces. Roll up chicken like a stuffed cabbage. Drizzle with 1 teaspoon olive oil and sprinkle with ground black pepper and Italian seasoning. Cover and bake at 350°F for 30 minutes, then uncover and broil for 5 minutes, or until lightly browned. Slice each roll into 3 pieces. (Have 6 pieces for dinner, the other pieces for day 15's lunch.)
1 cup steamed sugar snap peas

| 433 | 32.6 g | 45.5 g | 9 g |

| **TOTAL** | **1,557** | **189.5 g** (49%) | **102.9 g** (26%) | **41.1 g** (24%) |

{ I DID IT! } ‣

Name: Wanda Chen

Age: 36

Town: Sunnyvale, California

Weight Lost: 23 pounds

Other Accomplishments: Shrank from a size 12 to a size 8 and reduced her stress levels

before   after

"Before I got married in 1991, my weight had always held steady between 100 and 105 pounds. In 1998, I gave birth to my daughter, and my weight shot up to 135 pounds. Later, after I gave birth to my son, my weight climbed again, this time to 145 pounds. In June 2002, I quit my job, and my stress levels soared. In order to deal with my stress, I kept baking and eating my favorite dessert—chocolate chip cookies. I did about 10 minutes of exercise about 3 days a week. I hated to exercise.

"By September 2002, my weight was up to 155 pounds. I knew I had to do something. I began watching Denise's show on Lifetime the middle of that month. Two weeks later, I actually began exercising with Denise. At that time, I did not change my eating habits or drink much water; however, just the exercise helped me lose some weight. I then started keeping a food diary and counting calories. I was shocked to learn that I was eating at least 2,000 calories daily. I reduced my calorie consumption to between 1,200 and 1,500 a day. The weight and inches came off.

"Denise always keeps me motivated and has taught me to treat exercise as a daily appointment. Now, every day, I must have some form of exercise, even just 10 minutes. It makes me feel so good and releases my stress.

"In April 2003, I went to my doctor for a checkup. I hadn't visited him in 8 months, and we were both impressed when I stepped on the scale and it revealed that I had lost 10 pounds. I know that with Denise's encouragement and by eating healthy, I can reach my goal of losing another 20 pounds. Thank you so much, Denise! You are my role model and hero!"

Wanda's Advice: Lose weight for your benefit, not to please others. No matter whether it takes you 3 months or 3 years to achieve your goal, you will earn the benefit of lifelong health. Make healthful eating and exercise a daily appointment. Know that one day of slipping up is not the end of the world. You can start over at any time. Change one habit at a time, and success will follow.

DENISE'S DAILY WISDOM

As you move through the program, you may notice that your weight on the scale doesn't necessarily reflect the wonderful changes that you've made to your body. Because muscle weighs more than fat, some people find that the scale weight changes very little, even though their bodies definitely are shrinking in size. Muscle takes up much less room than fat, so that's why you can sculpt your body and lose a dress size without losing weight on the scale.

A great way to measure your progress as you exchange fat for new muscle is to use a scale that measures more than your weight. Some scales will also measure your body-fat percentage. As you firm up, your body-fat level will continue to drop, even if your actual weight remains steady. That way, you will be able to assess your success accurately.

In addition to using a scale that measures your body-fat percentage, you can keep track of your measurements. Hopefully, you used a flexible tape measure to jot down the circumference of your thighs, belly, and hips before you started your journey. If so, continue to do it again at regular intervals; if not, start now, and watch the inches fly off!

{ "Exercise and healthful eating are important, because you are worth it!" }

day
(14) THE DAILY DOZEN

**PILATES TUMMY TUCK
(PAGE 136)**

PILATES TWIST (PAGE 137)

MERMAID (PAGE 163)

HIP RELEASE (PAGE 124)

HIP STRETCH (PAGE 125)

**HAMSTRING STRETCH
(PAGE 126)**

FORWARD BEND (PAGE 166)

CHEST STRETCH (PAGE 130)

**SHOULDER STRETCH
(PAGE 128)**

WHEEL (PAGE 167)

CHILD'S POSE (PAGE 132)

KNEE SWAY (PAGE 169)

255

day

(14) YOUR EATING PLAN

	Calories	Carbohydrate	Protein	Fat

BREAKFAST

Breakfast BT (Bacon and Tomato) Sandwich:
Toast 1 whole wheat English muffin. Spread on 1 tablespoon light mayonnaise. Add sliced tomato and 3 slices broiled Canadian bacon.

	256	30 g	21 g	8 g

MIDMORNING
1 orange

	65	16.3 g	1.4 g	0.1 g

LUNCH

Lentil and Tomato Soup:
Heat 10½-ounce can lentil soup and add 4 ounces canned mushrooms and 8-ounce can flavored, diced tomatoes.
1 whole grain roll
½ cup low-fat cottage cheese

	470	66 g	32 g	4 g

MIDAFTERNOON
¼ cup almonds

	170	5 g	6 g	14 g

DINNER

Italian Vegetable Frittata:
Sauté 1 small zucchini, garlic, and ½ cup diced tomatoes in 1 teaspoon olive oil for about 5 minutes. Add 2 tablespoons chopped green olives. Beat 2 large eggs and 2 egg whites with a little water and season with salt, pepper, and Italian seasoning. Pour over the vegetables and cook until set. Sprinkle with 1 tablespoon Parmesan.

Mango Spinach Salad:
Combine 2 cups baby spinach and ½ mango. Toss with 2 tablespoons light vinaigrette with a little grated lemon rind added.

	584	58 g	29 g	18 g

TOTAL	**1,545**	**175.3 g** (45%)	**89.4 g** (23%)	**44.1 g** (26%)

{ I DID IT! } ▸

Name: Mary Tate

Age: 37

Town: Denver, Colorado

Weight Lost: 55 pounds

Other Accomplishments: Went from a size 16 to a size 2 and improved her confidence

before   after

"I used to weigh 160 pounds and wore a size 16. I watched Denise's show and thought that I would never be able to lose the weight. At only 5 feet 2 inches, I knew that I had to lose some weight, but I didn't know how.

"But something wonderful happened to me one day when I saw Denise on QVC, where she was selling her step aerobics video, step, and weights. I picked up the phone, ordered the products, and haven't been the same since. I started exercising with the video. At first I couldn't even finish 10 minutes. I gradually began to exercise for longer and longer, and eventually made it through the entire video. I was hooked.

"After 2 years of regular exercise, the weight came off, and I reached my goal. It was such an awesome feeling to get fit and to lose that stubborn weight and keep it off. Since then, I have used Denise's stability ball and just love it. The ball is such a versatile piece of equipment that it let me work on my abs, buns, inner and outer thighs, and upper body with a new set of challenges that brought great results.

"I am in better shape now after my second baby than I was when I got married 7 years ago. It's hard to get up some mornings, especially when the baby has kept me up at night or I'm up late trying to 'catch up' on tasks, but I love the feeling after I exercise. I have so much energy afterward. I now weigh 104 pounds and wear a size 2. I have kept the weight off for 11 years now and through two babies. I thank Denise for being such a wonderful motivator. She is my inspiration."

Mary's Advice: To prevent overeating, never deprive yourself. "I love ice cream, cookies, chips, and so on," she says, "but I use portion control to help me have my treats but not overeat them."

◀ · · · · · · · · · · · · · · · · · ·

WEEK 3

After completing week 2, you are now two-thirds of the way through this weight-loss jump start. Way to go! Completing your routines, following the menus, getting plenty of sleep, and drinking eight glasses of water a day are significant accomplishments. Be proud of yourself. You've overcome procrastination!

The journey is well worth the effort. Keep going. The feeling of accomplishment is one of the most wonderful sensations in the world. You are building the discipline needed to continue your new healthful changes for the rest of your life. Although your toning and stretching routines may not completely feel natural yet—you still have 1 more week to go until they become a habit— the healthy, fitter you is already inside you. Your body, mind, and soul are slowly becoming accustomed to this new way of life. You are balancing your life from the inside out, and you are creating the dedication and type of lifestyle needed to be successful at everything you do, from your career aspirations to your family life.

In the coming week, your toning routines will become slightly more difficult. If you encounter an exercise that feels too challenging, move back to the less-challenging version of that exercise. For example, if, on day 16, you struggle to do just one pushup on one leg, you can return to the version with both legs on the ball.

Again, don't beat yourself up or feel discouraged. Attempt the more difficult version, see how well you do, and then do the less-challenging version if needed. Always remember this: The more you challenge yourself, the more your balance and coordination will improve. You'll see and feel the results.

If you need to lose more than 10 pounds, step up your cardio this week from 24 to 36 minutes, three to four times a week. Remember, you can do your cardio on any day you like, as long as you do it!

Continue to monitor your water intake and your hours of sleep—keep them up, up, up! Until you form your new, healthful habits, it can be too easy to slide back to those old ways. Writing down what you eat and drink and taking note of how many hours you sleep will keep you on track and accountable to yourself.

This week, when you focus on quality, think of how each deliberate movement in your plan brings you one step closer to your goals. By choosing to give each exercise your best effort, you're packing more value into every moment. Your time is your most precious resource—make it count!

You'll start your week with your day off, weigh-in, and preparation for the week to come. Keep an open mind and a positive outlook. You're almost there.

DENISE'S DAILY WISDOM

Everyone who knows me knows that I don't leave home without my trusty water bottle. I keep a bottle of water with me at all times and drink from it as often as possible. Drinking plenty of fluid helps fuel your energy levels, lower your appetite, and add a lustrous glow to your skin. When you become dehydrated, your blood becomes thicker, making your heart work twice as hard to pump it through your body. As your heart rate speeds up, you begin to feel fatigued while performing common everyday tasks.

Dehydration is not at all an ideal state in which to perform your exercise routines. You'll breathe harder than usual. Also, your body will have a tougher time regulating your temperature. Finally, dehydration often causes a dull headache and fatigue.

The best thing about water is that it contains zero calories. It doesn't matter whether you drink club soda with a wedge of lemon or lime or plain tap water, as long as you drink eight glasses a day. I recommend you use water bottles, because you can take them with you in the car and on errands and other trips away from home, ensuring that you'll never get dehydrated.

{ "Supercharge your fat-burning power by keeping up with your muscle-conditioning exercises. Muscles work miracles on your metabolism." }

day

(15) THE DAILY DOZEN

Day Off!

Today is your day off from exercise. Enjoy your day and be grateful for your accomplishments during the past week. Feel good about yourself for how far you've come. Reward yourself with a bubble bath, a massage, a manicure, or some other treat. Allow your body the luxury and necessity of rest and renewal.

Weigh-In

You're doing great! Take a moment to chart your progress.

- ▶ Your current weight

- ▶ Your current measurements

- ▶ Your other accomplishments (such as a compliment from a friend or a resisted temptation)

Reflection

Before you head into your final week, take a moment to ponder the following.

1. What did you do well last week?

2. How could you improve your motivation and dedication?

3. Set one goal that you plan to accomplish in the coming week. (For example, increase your cardio by 12 minutes, or try to increase the number of repetitions in your workouts by one or two.)

Preparation

Spend time today preparing for the week to come. Shop for the items on your shopping list today. Then, complete any preparatory tasks that will help make the rest of your week go more smoothly. For example, you might cook the stuffed peppers for day 19's dinner and freeze them, so you just have to defrost them and pop them in the microwave oven to make dinner.

day

(15) YOUR EATING PLAN

	Calories	Carbohydrate	Protein	Fat

BREAKFAST

Breakfast Parfait:
Combine ½ cup low-fat cottage cheese, ½ cup high-fiber cereal, and ½ cup frozen berries.

Calories	Carbohydrate	Protein	Fat
181	30 g	17 g	2 g

MIDMORNING
1 kiwifruit

| 46 | 11.3 g | 0.8 g | 0.3 g |

LUNCH

Stuffed Chicken Salad:
Toss 2 cups mixed greens with 2 tablespoons light vinaigrette. Add ½ cup canned chickpeas, flavored with a little cumin powder. Top with 6 slices cold stuffed chicken breast (from day 13's dinner).

| 505 | 48.3 g | 34 g | 19 g |

MIDAFTERNOON
½ cup bean dip
1 red pepper, cut into thin strips for dipping

| 120 | 20.7 g | 9 g | 0.1 g |

DINNER

Spinach Cheese Tortellini with Feta, Tomatoes, Salmon, and Pesto:
Prepare 1 package spinach cheese tortellini according to package directions. Add 2 cups grape tomatoes, a 3-ounce can salmon (drained), and ¼ cup crumbled feta. Stir in 2 tablespoons pesto. (Have half for dinner, the other half for day 16's lunch.)
1 cup steamed sugar snap peas

| 705 | 75.9 g | 49.9 g | 25.9 g |

	Calories	Carbohydrate	Protein	Fat
TOTAL	**1,557**	**186.2 g** (48%)	**110.7 g** (28%)	**47.3 g** (27%)

{ I DID IT! } ▸

Name: Suzie Wilson

Age: 40

Town: Steilacoom, Washington

Weight Lost: 65 pounds

Other Accomplishments: Shrank from a size 18 to a size 10 and has maintained the weight loss for 6 years

before   after

"I have been overweight for most of my life, using food as a source of comfort. After the birth of my daughter, Heather, in 1993, my health began to deteriorate as a consequence of my excess weight. I developed gallbladder problems and low immunity. My doctor warned that if I didn't lose weight, I would probably develop cardiac problems or diabetes. He said that losing the extra weight would help me regain my health. I wasn't interested in any of the fad diets, as I knew that I had to make a lifestyle change. I felt scared and knew I needed to make serious changes.

"A friend of mine told me about Denise, so I tried out one of her workouts. Between exercising with Denise at least four times per week, taking daily walks with my coworkers, and eating five small meals per day, the weight fell off. It took a little longer than a year to lose the weight, tone up, and regain my health. I then embarked on my maintenance program.

"Attempting to manage a household, be a wife and mother, work 24 hours each week, and attend college full-time is challenging. I work out each morning and find time throughout each day to incorporate wall pushups, triceps toners, leg exercises, and situps, or go for an invigorating walk.

"Denise has helped me in several ways. Her smile just brightens my day. She has inspired me to continue exercising and eating healthfully, so I'm taking better care of my health. I emulate her motivation for being positive by encouraging my coworkers and my friends with their goals.

"My recent glucose and cholesterol panels were perfect. I am very thankful that I listened to my friend who told me about Denise and her workouts. Denise is truly a positive role model for the world to follow. She sets the example and follows through. Thank you, Denise!"

Suzie's Advice: Extra weight does not show up overnight. It takes months, possibly years, to put on, so do not expect the weight to drop off overnight. The slower the process, the more likely the results will last. Lose 1 pound at a time. Eventually, you will reach your goal.

DENISE'S DAILY WISDOM

If you've been having a hard time losing weight and you've thoroughly examined your diet, you may want to take a closer look at your liquid sources of calories. I find that many people drink many more calories than they realize, and most people don't think of soft drinks and fruit juices in the same way they think of hamburgers and french fries. Yet, the soft drink often may have more calories than the hamburger!

Always check the Nutrition Facts label on soft drinks and other caloric beverages. Make sure to check the serving size. Many drinks actually count as two or more servings, which means you must multiply the amount of calories by the number of servings to find out the true number of calories in the bottle. You may be surprised to learn that your healthy bottle of juice contains 200 or more calories—calories that could be hindering your weight-loss efforts! Also, never order a supersize drink, unless it's water.

{ "When you finish a workout,
you don't simply feel better,
you feel better about yourself!" }

day

(16) THE DAILY DOZEN

1

**UPPER-BACK STRETCH
(PAGE 116)**

2

**INTERMEDIATE FRENCH
CURL (PAGE 107)**

3

**UPPER-BACK FIRMER
(PAGE 91)**

4

**INTERMEDIATE WALL SQUAT
(PAGE 61)**

5

BALL TAP (PAGE 62)

6

**ADVANCED PUSHUP
(PAGE 89)**

7

**INTERMEDIATE LATERAL
RAISE (PAGE 95)**

8

**INTERMEDIATE BICEPS
CURL (PAGE 109)**

9

CHEST STRETCH (PAGE 130)

10

**ADVANCED BALL SQUEEZE
(PAGE 67)**

11

**LOWER-BODY TONER
(PAGE 68)**

12

**ADVANCED BOTTOMS-UP
(PAGE 66)**

16 YOUR EATING PLAN

	Calories	Carbohydrate	Protein	Fat

BREAKFAST

Mexican Egg Sandwich:
Fry 1 large egg in vegetable spray. Place in a whole wheat flour tortilla spread with 2 tablespoons salsa and a little chopped jalapeño (if desired).
1 tangerine

| | 244 | 34.4 g | 10 g | 5.6 g |

MIDMORNING

1 pear

| | 98 | 25.1 g | 0.7 g | 0.7 g |

LUNCH

Tortellini Salad:
Toss cold leftover tortellini with ½ sliced cucumber and 1 small pepper cut into rings or strips.

| | 704 | 74.9 g | 49.9 g | 25.9 g |

MIDAFTERNOON

8 ounces light yogurt

| | 100 | 16 g | 6 g | 0 g |

DINNER

Foil-Baked Herbed Chicken Breast:
Wrap in foil 1 chicken breast (7 ounces raw weight) with chopped green onions, 1 tablespoon capers, 1 teaspoon dill weed, 2 thin lemon slices, and 1 teaspoon olive oil. Bake for 30 minutes at 350°F.
Roasted Vegetables:
Place ½ cup each of zucchini, mushrooms, red onion, and broccoli in a baking dish, and toss with 1 teaspoon olive oil and a splash of balsamic vinegar. Bake uncovered at 425°F for 30 minutes.

| | 377 | 10.3 g | 43.5 g | 15.5 g |

| **TOTAL** | **1,523** | **160.7 g** (42%) | **110.1 g** (29%) | **47.7 g** (28%) |

{ I DID IT! } ▸

Name: DiAnn Boehm

Age: 39

Town: Ames, Nebraska

Weight Lost: 30 pounds

Other Accomplishments: Shrank two clothing sizes and boosted her energy and stamina

before   after

"I've struggled with my weight my entire life. I would lose it, gain it, lose it, and gain it. After giving birth to my third son, I weighed 188 pounds and began trying to lose weight yet again. I had been thinking of getting serious about weight loss for some time, but it wasn't until a friend said she joined an online weight-loss group that I took the plunge. She inspired me, and I thought we could help each other on our weight-loss journey.

"In July 2002, I started being diligent about my diet and working out every day. I rode my exercise bike or worked out on the stairclimber. I slowly eliminated refined sugars, caffeine, dairy products, and most fatty meats. I began drinking lots of water, too. I had some success, but it wasn't until I started exercising with Denise during her two morning workouts on Lifetime that I really began to see results. That is when I started to tone and firm and noticed my dress sizes going down. Then I saw major improvement in my post-childbirth body with Denise's Pilates exercises, some of which incorporated the band. I've had three C-sections, so I never dreamed that my tummy could look so toned!

"It still needs work, but I'm very excited at how every part of my body is firming up.

"I have more energy and stamina. I feel better about myself—and it must show. What I put out into the world is positive and friendly, and it's amazing how people reciprocate! I always remember what Denise says, 'God gave you one body—it's up to you to take care of it' and 'Strong bodies equal strong minds, and you are worth it!'"

DiAnn's Advice: Learn to speak nicely to yourself. Admire your body for what it can do. Learn to accept yourself and realize that you are a work in progress. Keep promises you make to yourself. Hiding to eat food doesn't hide the food from your body.

◂ · · · · · · · · · · · · · · · · ·

day 17
(Tuesday)

DENISE'S DAILY WISDOM

Have you ever had one of those days when you meant to eat right and fit in exercise, but everything seemed to conspire against you? Perhaps you meant to get up early, but when the alarm went off, you slept just a little longer. And then when you got up, your day started with a bang and didn't end until 10 hours later. You found yourself rushing around and getting by on snack chips and junk. By the time you came home, you raided the fridge, and then when you were done, you were mad at yourself. Don't worry, these types of days happen to me, too.

The important thing to remember is that it's over. Tomorrow is a brand-new day. Think positive and start with a clean slate. Calmly try to learn from such days. What could you have done differently? At any point during the day could you have put your needs ahead of the needs of others? How can you prevent such occurrences in the future? Learn from it, move on, and promise to treat yourself with greater respect in the future. One of the ways I prevent myself from slipping up is with careful planning. I prepare bags of healthy foods such as nuts, fruit, and so on. That way I can turn to these healthful snacks instead of junk.

{ "Eating right isn't about willpower.
It's about changing bad habits." }

day

(17) THE DAILY DOZEN

WAIST ROTATION/LOWER-BACK STRETCH (PAGE 117)

HIP RELEASE (PAGE 124)

ADVANCED CRUNCH (PAGE 37)

ADVANCED OBLIQUE TWIST (PAGE 39)

BACK STRETCH (PAGE 35)

ADVANCED PLANK (PAGE 45)

ADVANCED RISE AND SHINE (PAGE 53)

RECIPROCAL REACH (PAGE 54)

T-STAND (PAGE 140)

LOWER-TUMMY FIRMER (PAGE 41)

TEASER (PAGE 146)

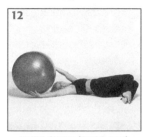

KNEE SWAY (PAGE 169)

269

WEEK 3

day

(17) **YOUR EATING PLAN**

	Calories	Carbohydrate	Protein	Fat
BREAKFAST				
2 whole grain waffles 2 tablespoons light syrup 2 slices Canadian bacon ½ grapefruit	366	57.4 g	17.6 g	9.5 g
MIDMORNING				
1 medium kiwifruit	46	11.3 g	0.8 g	0.3 g
LUNCH				
Salmon Salad: Combine 2 cups mixed greens with ½ cucumber and ½ pepper. Toss with 2 tablespoons light dressing, whisked with 1 teaspoon mustard and ½ teaspoon horseradish. Add a 3-ounce can of salmon, flavored with a little Old Bay seasoning and 1 teaspoon capers. 1 whole grain roll	420	33.6 g	28.8 g	16.1 g
MIDAFTERNOON				
2 pieces light string cheese	120	0 g	14 g	6 g
DINNER				
Pork Loin with Barley: Bake 1 pork loin (6 ounces raw weight), sprinkled with fresh rosemary and garlic, at 350°F for 30 minutes, turning over halfway through. Or sauté in pan for 15 minutes, with a little chicken or onion broth, until both sides are browned. Cook barley (¼ cup dry) in either chicken or onion broth. Add ½ cup mushrooms sautéed in 1 tablespoon whipped butter. 10 spears steamed asparagus	576	45 g	44.7 g	15.1 g
TOTAL	**1,528**	**147.3 g** (39%)	**105.9 g** (28%)	**47 g** (28%)

{ I DID IT! } ▸

Name: Susan Cooperstock

Age: 35

Town: Columbia, Missouri

Weight Lost: 10 pounds

Other Accomplishments: Lost 10 inches and became stronger and more flexible

before　　　　after

"I had been thin my entire life, mostly because of my chronic ulcerative colitis. After multiple abdominal surgeries, I finally began to get healthy. With that health, however, came additional pounds— some needed, but some not! Because of all the surgeries and long hospital stays, I had also lost a great deal of muscle, which slowed my metabolism.

"I discovered Denise's Pilates program and the stability ball 4 months ago. Because my abdominal muscles were weak from 10 surgeries, I decided to zero in on that area of my body. My abdomen was so weak that I could not do traditional floor exercises. I felt successful on the ball because it gave me the support I needed to strengthen my abdomen slowly. I love Denise's positive attitude so much.

"I am still working to become healthy and strong through gradual changes. I now do Denise's yoga and Pilates 4 days a week along with walking. I'd still like to firm up more, but I am astonished at how much stronger and more flexible I have become. My husband, friends, and physicians are amazed at how healthy I seem and how strong I am.

"I recently hiked more than 60 miles in 1 week. It is wonderful to feel that sense of accomplishment after years of serious illness. My body has finally become strong and healthy again!"

Susan's Advice: Each week replace one or two poor eating habits with a healthy habit. For example, one week replace fast food with a healthy eating choice at lunchtime. Instead of skipping breakfast, sip on a smoothie during your commute to work. In the same way, gradually implement more exercise into your life. Start with just 10 minutes a day, and add more time from there. "You can't change your entire lifestyle overnight," she says. "You must set goals, identify what you want to change, and then go do it!"

◂ ·

DENISE'S DAILY WISDOM

Many people ask me to recommend a set of exercises that will help create more energy. There is no shortage of things you can do to create more energy, but I start by asking people about their sleep and relaxation habits before going further. Often, I find that they need more energy because they routinely get by on less than 7 hours of sleep. Although exercise, a healthy diet, and plenty of water will certainly help energize you, they are not solutions for lack of sleep.

I recommend that you go to bed at the same time every night and get up at the same time every morning. Try to wind down for an hour before bed by doing some light reading or stretching. Then plan to hit the sack around 10:00 P.M. on weekday nights and sleep for 8 hours. Only then can you expect to create more energy by exercising and eating healthful foods.

{ "Relish this feeling of satisfaction that you can only get from knowing that you are taking care of yourself." }

HUG-A-BALL (PAGE 115)

INTERMEDIATE WARRIOR 1
(PAGE 157)

ADVANCED PUSHUP
(PAGE 89)

BACK AND SHOULDER
FIRMER (PAGE 99)

INTERMEDIATE UPRIGHT
ROW (PAGE 101)

ADVANCED FRENCH CURL
(PAGE 107)

CHEST STRETCH (PAGE 130)

INTERMEDIATE BICEPS
CURL (PAGE 109)

DEADLIFT (PAGE 71)

BACK-OF-THIGH TONER
(PAGE 74)

HIP CIRCLES (PAGE 142)

OUTER-THIGH TONER
(PAGE 69)

18 YOUR EATING PLAN

	Calories	Carbohydrate	Protein	Fat
BREAKFAST 1 cup high-fiber cereal 8 ounces fat-free milk ½ cup fresh or frozen blueberries	271	61 g	12.5 g	1.3 g
MIDMORNING ¼ cup sunflower seeds	165	7 g	5 g	14 g
LUNCH 2 slices whole grain bread 2 tablespoons crunchy peanut butter 1 tangerine	387	39 g	14.5 g	18.2 g
MIDAFTERNOON ½ cup low-fat plain yogurt mixed with 2 tablespoons onion soup mix Thinly sliced zucchini for dipping	124	18.4 g	7.3 g	1.4 g
DINNER **Ginger Teriyaki Tuna with Bulgur:** Spoon 2 to 3 tablespoons ginger teriyaki sauce on 6 ounces fresh tuna. Broil 7 to 8 minutes per side. Cook bulgur (½ cup dry) in chicken broth, with some toasted onion and a dash of dill. 1 cup green beans, steamed and tossed with ½ cup flavored, diced tomatoes	609	51.2 g	65 g	11 g
TOTAL	1,556	176.6 g (45%)	104.3 g (27%)	45.9 g (27%)

{ I DID IT! } ▸

Name: Paula Shupe

Age: 29

Town: Lebanon, Ohio

Weight Lost: 42 pounds

Other Accomplishments: Boosted her energy and mood

before   after

"During my pregnancy with my second baby, I gained 42 pounds. People say that if you gain over 40 pounds during a pregnancy, you probably won't be able to lose it all once you have the baby. I had my baby on March 24, 2003, but didn't get the okay from my doctor to exercise until May 12. I started out with Denise's book *Lose Those Last 10 Pounds* and then substituted a few favorite recipes from another of her books, *Jump Start.*

"I lost 9 pounds in 4 weeks and was motivated to keep going. Every weekday morning, I work out with Denise's TV shows. On Mondays, Wednesdays, and Fridays, I also do an hour of Pilates. On Tuesdays and Thursdays, I do 20 minutes of Pilates, and I rotate one of my favorite workout tapes. On Saturdays and Sundays, I take a 30-minute walk. As Denise suggests, I keep my calories around 1,500 and snack twice a day—and I *never* feel hungry.

"At the end of August, I stepped on the scale and found that I had lost all 42 pounds! Denise inspires me with her positive attitude, energy, tips about fitness and nutrition, and I love working out with her every day. Often, my infant son will be screaming in the background while I'm working out, and my 2-year-old daughter is crying for my attention. But I know that if I don't get those workouts in, I won't be the best mommy I can be—I'll be impatient and irritable and find myself getting frustrated more easily.

"I'm a completely different person on the days I don't exercise. Denise's energy and enthusiasm make me feel so positive and happy to be alive. Thanks, Denise, for all you've taught me!"

Paula's Advice: "Fidgetcise" by spending 1 minute of every hour in some form of movement. It will curb your appetite, keep you energized, and help you tone all of your problem areas. Plus, you'll get a bonus 15 minutes of exercise in during the day without feeling like you are exercising.

DENISE'S DAILY WISDOM

From time to time, I hear from women and men who complain, "I hardly eat any-thing, but I still can't lose weight." I ask them what they are eating, and they tell me something like, "I have an orange for breakfast, a cup of yogurt for lunch, and a salad for dinner." Often when I pursue it a bit further, I find out that they raid the fridge at some point after 8:00 P.M. and end up consuming the bulk of their calories at night—often more calories than they ate all day long.

Skipping meals and starving yourself can be as detrimental as consistently eating too much. First, your body senses that your calorie intake is low and auto-matically slows down your metabolism as a result. Second, when you feel hungry all day long, you will eventually give in to the urge and end up eating much more food than you would have if you had eaten three meals and two healthy snacks during the day. The menus in this program contain the perfect mix of the right types of food to help spur weight loss without slowing your metabolism or making you crave calories.

{ "Posture speaks volumes.
Make sure yours says, 'confidence.'" }

day

(19) THE DAILY DOZEN

1

UPPER-BACK STRETCH
(PAGE 116)

2

ADVANCED PLANK
(PAGE 45)

3

COBRA (PAGE 164)

4

LOWER-BACK
STRENGTHENER (PAGE 51)

5

INTERMEDIATE TORSO
TONER (PAGE 40)

6

BACK STRETCH (PAGE 35)

7

INTERMEDIATE CRUNCH
(PAGE 37)

8

ADVANCED OBLIQUE TWIST
(PAGE 39)

9

NATURAL TUMMY TUCK
(PAGE 46)

10

DOUBLE-LEG STRETCH
(PAGE 148)

11

INTERMEDIATE BICYCLE
(PAGE 49)

12

KNEE SWAY (PAGE 169)

day

(19) YOUR EATING PLAN

	Calories	Carbohydrate	Protein	Fat

BREAKFAST
1 whole grain English muffin
1 tablespoon peanut butter
8 ounces light yogurt

305	43.5 g	15 g	9 g

MIDMORNING
½ grapefruit

46	11.9 g	0.6 g	0.1 g

LUNCH
10¾-ounce can of vegetable soup with
2 tablespoons dry barley added
Portobello Mushrooms:
  Sauté 2 mushrooms in 1 teaspoon olive
  oil until tender, or 5 to 7 minutes, with
  a splash of balsamic vinegar. Top with
  2 slices provolone cheese.

509	57.1 g	28.9 g	19.3 g

MIDAFTERNOON
½ cup salsa
Sliced sweet red, yellow, or green pepper
for dipping

60	12.8 g	2.7 g	0.1 g

DINNER
Stuffed Peppers:
  Cook ¼ cup brown rice in tomato juice.
  Brown ½ pound ground turkey breast with
  1 tablespoon olive oil, 1 chopped medium
  onion, and a dash of cayenne and chili
  powder to taste. Mix ground turkey into the
  rice. Stuff the rice-turkey mixture into 2
  large red or green peppers. Place peppers
  in a pan, with ¼" water in the bottom.
  Cover with foil and bake at 350°F for 20
  minutes, or until peppers are tender.
Spinach Salad:
  Combine 1 cup baby spinach and ½ cup
  strawberries. Toss with 1 tablespoon
  raspberry-flavored vinaigrette.

555	55.7 g	47.9 g	17.3 g

TOTAL:	**1,475**	**181 g** (49%)	**95.1 g** (26%)	**45.8 g** (28%)

{ I DID IT! } ▸

Name: Karen Gaskill

Age: 30

Town: Port Deposit, Maryland

Weight Lost: 87 pounds

Other Accomplishments: Went from a size 22 to a size 6 and changed her body and life

before   after

"I gained weight before and during my three pregnancies, mostly because of a flawed, low-fat diet. I ate a lot of pasta, thinking that it was low fat but not taking into account the sheer volume of food I was consuming. I was also an avid soda drinker, consuming six to eight sodas a day. Everyone always laughed at me because I was the one walking around with the Super Big Gulp cup in hand at all times. I was also a fast-food junkie, always ordering the Extra Value Meal with a Coke.

"I wasn't happy with myself and felt tired and winded often. At age 30, I decided that I was not going to be this same weight by my 31st birthday. I began exercising regularly and eating a balanced, healthy diet. No more TV dinners—I would eat whole grains, fruits, and vegetables from now on. I also wanted to teach myself the correct way to exercise. I started working out with Denise, and I fell in love with the art of yoga and Pilates. Those disciplines have changed my body and life.

"I have learned that balance is the key to success. It has taken me 8 months of exercising 6 days a week to reach my goal. I will be 31 in a month and have gone from a size 22 to a size 6 and have lost 87 pounds. My energy level is up. I now feel more centered and healthier in everything I do.

"Everyone has been so loving and supportive of me losing weight. My husband helps to keep the kids busy so that I can exercise. My family has encouraged me all along. I used to turn to them for advice about weight loss. Now they turn to me. Not long ago, a friend whom I had not seen in ages walked up to me and asked me my name. She said she could hardly recognize me because I looked so toned."

Karen's Advice: Take time for yourself to do all exercise practices. You need to stretch for flexibility, exercise aerobically for fat burning, and do a form of resistance training to strengthen and tone your muscles. Try many different forms of exercise, from yoga and Pilates to tennis and powerwalking. Each type of exercise will reshape your body in ways that no one exercise can do.

day 20
(Friday)

DENISE'S DAILY WISDOM

Do you ever feel frustrated when your tummy begins to rumble only an hour or so after you've eaten breakfast? It seems as if your body burned through your morning meal at an exceptionally fast rate, and depending on what you ate, it probably did.

Many of us turn to carbohydrates first thing in the morning, in the form of cold cereal, a bagel, or a muffin. Pure carbohydrate, however, usually isn't enough to fend off hunger until your midmorning snack time. Of all the macronutrients—carbohydrates, protein, and fats—your body digests and uses carbohydrates the quickest. You can keep the morning munchies at bay by adding a bit of protein or some healthful fats to your morning meal. Try mixing a little peanut butter in your oatmeal both for flavor and staying power. Or, have a hard-cooked egg along with your morning fruit. Try a fruit smoothie made with Egg Beaters or some other egg substitute—because egg substitutes are pasteurized, you can dump them into your smoothie without cooking them.

{ "When you approach an activity with belief in yourself, you will perform beyond your expectations!" }

MERMAID (PAGE 163)

ADVANCED PUSHUP
(PAGE 89)

ADVANCED ARM ROW
(PAGE 93)

FLOOR TAP (PAGE 63)

BALL TAP (PAGE 62)

ADVANCED OVERHEAD
PRESS (PAGE 103)

SHOULDER STRETCH
(PAGE 128)

ROWING SERIES (PAGE 150)

ARM STRETCH (PAGE 131)

BICEPS CURL (PAGE 108)

THIGH SHAPER (PAGE 78)

CHILD'S POSE (PAGE 132)

day

20 YOUR EATING PLAN

	Calories	Carbohydrate	Protein	Fat

BREAKFAST

Berry Smoothie:
  Blend 8 ounces fat-free milk, 4 ounces
  silken tofu, and 1 cup frozen berries.
**1 slice whole grain toast with 1
tablespoon peanut butter**

	341	40.9 g	22 g	12.3 g

MIDMORNING
1 orange

65	16.3 g	1.4 g	0.1 g

LUNCH

**1 frozen light entrée (chicken or beef
stir-fry)**
Marinated Vegetable Salad:
  Toss 1 cup chunky frozen vegetables with
  2 tablespoons light vinaigrette and some
  finely chopped parsley.

	351	34.5 g	22.2 g	11 g

MIDAFTERNOON
3 tablespoons popcorn (air-popped)

110	16 g	3 g	4 g

DINNER

Tomato-Topped Roughy:
  Grill or broil an 8-ounce piece of roughy for
  5 to 7 minutes and top with a mixture of
  flavored, diced tomatoes; ½ finely chopped
  shallot; and a little lemon rind.
Penne with Ricotta and Spinach:
  Cook ¾ cup (dry) whole wheat penne
  pasta. Toss with ½ cup part-skim ricotta
  cheese, 1 tablespoon Parmesan cheese,
  and ½ cup lightly steamed spinach.
10 spears steamed asparagus

	697	55.6 g	78.6 g	17.2 g

TOTAL	Calories	Carbohydrate	Protein	Fat
	1,564	163.3 g (42%)	127.2 g (33%)	44.6 g (26%)

{ I DID IT! } ▸

Name: Debbie Herbert

Age: 45

Town: Wetumpka, Alabama

Weight Lost: 10 pounds

Other Accomplishments: Shrank from a size 8 to a size 6

before   after

"Over the years, I have typically gained a few pounds during the holiday season and then slimmed back down during January. Last Christmas, I gained more than usual and failed to lose the weight come January. I developed a huge appetite for sugars and starches. My clothes became tight, and I began feeling lethargic.

"I decided to jump-start my day by working out with Denise every morning before I went to work. Denise kept me motivated and fueled my desire to get as healthy and fit as possible. One day she mentioned that she was starting a discussion group on her Web site for viewers to share tips on weight loss and support one another in the process. I logged on as soon as I could.

"I have learned so much from her forum on www.deniseaustin.com and have found the wisdom and motivation to lose all of the weight. Some people say that being 10 pounds overweight is no big deal. Some people say that you should *expect* to be slightly overweight once you hit your forties. I say that, for me, being at my ideal weight and developing muscle has done more to enhance my self-image and confidence level than anything I have ever done. I have tons more energy, too.

"Now that I've lost the weight, I want to develop stronger muscles and more flexibility. To me, it's not just about maintaining a certain weight on the scale, it's also about building my body to its fullest potential. I will maintain this lifestyle so that I can enjoy my future retirement, grandchildren, 25-year wedding anniversary, and whatever other blessings await me."

Debbie's Advice: Whenever you feel discouraged or lack motivation, focus on the mental benefits of exercise. Regular exercise helps boost your confidence and self-esteem. "I think of my workouts as a self-esteem booster," she says. "Exercise physically gives my body a shot of endorphins, while mentally it makes me feel proud and confident." Your sense of accomplishment will build with every workout as you see the results on your body.

◂

DENISE'S DAILY WISDOM

Have you noticed that some stretches or toning exercises feel easier on one side of your body than the other? As most of us are right- or left-handed, we tend to use that hand more often than the other. That sets up a strength imbalance in our upper bodies. For example, if you are right-handed, the muscles in your right arm are probably stronger than the muscles in your left arm. Similarly, most of us preferentially use one leg more than the other. Finally, little habits that we do over and over all day long without noticing, such as crossing our legs, can tighten muscles on one side of the body more than the other. And certain sports that emphasize one side of the body will do the same.

So, what should you do about it? If you notice a strength imbalance, you can try to do more reps on your weaker side. If you notice a flexibility imbalance, you can hold a stretch on your weaker side for a longer period of time or repeat twice on that side and only once on the more flexible side.

{ "Food isn't the enemy.
Sitting still is!
Get going. You'll feel great." }

PILATES TUMMY TUCK
(PAGE 136)

FRONT-OF-THIGH STRETCH
(PAGE 123)

POSE OF THE DANCER
(PAGE 155)

SAW (PAGE 138)

MERMAID (PAGE 163)

HIP RELEASE (PAGE 124)

HIP STRETCH (PAGE 125)

HAMSTRING STRETCH
(PAGE 126)

CHEST STRETCH (PAGE 130)

SHOULDER STRETCH
(PAGE 128)

CHILD'S POSE (PAGE 132)

KNEE SWAY (PAGE 169)

day

(21) **YOUR EATING PLAN**

	Calories	Carbohydrate	Protein	Fat
BREAKFAST				
1 cup high-fiber cereal 8 ounces light yogurt 1 cup fresh or frozen strawberries	298	60.2 g	11 g	1.6 g
MIDMORNING				
1 pear	98	25 g	0.7 g	0.7 g
LUNCH				
Onion and Mushroom Omelet: Whisk 2 large eggs and 2 egg whites. Sauté ¼ cup canned mushrooms and ½ small chopped onion in a little butter-flavored spray. Remove from pan. Spray pan again and add beaten eggs. Cook until almost set, add the vegetables, fold over eggs, and cook until set. Splash hot pepper sauce to taste. 1 baked Idaho potato (4" × 2") with a little butter-flavored spray ½ grapefruit	359	40 g	25 g	11 g
MIDAFTERNOON				
¼ cup almonds	170	5 g	6 g	14 g
DINNER				
Chicken Quesadillas: Top each of 2 toasted corn tortillas with ¼ cup black beans, 4 ounces cooked skinless chicken (flavored with chili powder), 2 tablespoons salsa, shredded lettuce, and ¼ cup shredded light Cheddar cheese.	666	54.4 g	76 g	16.2 g
TOTAL	**1,591**	**184.6 g** (46%)	**118.7 g** (30%)	**43.5 g** (25%)

{ I DID IT! } ▸

Name: Barbara Nicholson

Age: 38

Town: Elmira Heights, New York

Weight Lost: 25 pounds

Other Accomplishments: Shrank from a size 12 to a size 4

before   after

"I began gaining weight when I reached puberty. I ate a fairly healthful diet but overindulged in too many treats and didn't get enough exercise. I ballooned to a size 14. During my third year in college, I enrolled in a police tactics course. In that class, I learned about conditioning my heart and lungs for physical strength. As I began to exercise regularly, my body started to change for the better—and it felt great. I later graduated and became a police officer.

"Two years later, I got pregnant with my first child. I read everything I could find on having a healthy pregnancy and birth. That is when I started exercising with Denise.

"I've returned to a size 8 after each of my five pregnancies. My oldest is now 15; my youngest, 3. The nutritional and exercise information that I learned from Denise helped me to raise healthy and happy children.

"After my last child was done nursing, I began to really focus on incorporating different exercises that Denise introduced to me, such as Pilates, yoga, and walking. With the new forms of exercise, I shrank to a size 4 and lost 25 more pounds. I now feel great. I have been told numerous times that I look much younger than my age. I've been asked how I do it, and my reply is always 'Denise!'

"If it weren't for Denise's enthusiasm and expertise, I would not have the energy or fit body required to take care of my family. I've gone from a size 12 to a size 4 with her advice. Daily exercise and healthy choices for food have made all the difference."

Barbara's Advice: Make exercise a daily healthy habit and stick with it. When you exercise on a regular basis, you will pass on your healthy habits to those around you, such as your spouse and children.

◂ . . . .

DENISE'S DAILY WISDOM

Congratulations!

You did it! You've completed your Daily Dozen program, 21 days of getting your body and mind in better shape. Give yourself a standing ovation! You are a winner. You made a decision to improve your lifestyle, and you've accomplished that goal. I'm so proud of you.

I know this is the beginning of a new chapter in *you*, one in which you take care of yourself, give yourself the time to renew and recharge, and carve out some time every day—even if it's just 12 minutes—to give your body the exercise it craves.

{ "Think positive and be optimistic. Going through the motions can trigger the emotions!" }

day
22 THE DAILY DOZEN

Day Off!

Appreciate your success. You've earned it! It's very important to acknowledge your accomplishments when you've done well. This positive reinforcement will help you to turn your 3-week triumph into a lifetime of good, healthy choices about enjoying movement and feeding your body the quality food it deserves.

Weigh-In

Take a (fun!) moment to assess your progress after your initial program.

▶ Your current weight

▶ Your current measurements

▶ Your other accomplishments here (such as swearing off afternoon chocolate or moving down a size in clothing)

Reflection

Today you have the perfect opportunity to ponder how the 3-week program will help you get a head start on your long-term goals.

1. What did you do well over the past few weeks?

2. What challenges did you face?

3. How can you learn from those challenges in the future?

4. What new goals can you make to help keep you motivated?

You're on the right path of healthful eating and regular exercise. From this day forward, this book offers a number of options. You can continue to cycle through the 3-week plan, moving back to day 1 and using the suggested exercises and menus. Or, you can use what you have learned during the past few weeks to design your own routines (see chapter 9) and menus.

The choice is yours. Stay on the path and keep it up. You are worth it!

day

22 YOUR EATING PLAN

	Calories	Carbohydrate	Protein	Fat
BREAKFAST				
Crunchy Cinnamon Oatmeal: Oatmeal (1 packet or ½ cup dry) with 4 ounces fat-free milk. Stir in 2 tablespoons light syrup, 2 tablespoons chopped almonds, and 1 small finely chopped apple. Sprinkle with cinnamon.	416	68 g	12.5 g	12.5 g
MIDMORNING 1 orange	65	16.3 g	1.4 g	0.1 g
LUNCH				
Turkey Wrap: Wrap 4 ounces smoked turkey breast, lettuce, and sliced tomato in a whole wheat pita with raspberry mustard.	366	39.7 g	30 g	8.4 g
MIDAFTERNOON **Hearty Dip:** Blend together ½ cup low-fat cottage cheese and 4 ounces tofu. Add 2 tablespoons vegetable soup mix. **Radishes and ½ peeled cucumber for dipping**	180	14 g	24 g	1.5 g
DINNER				
Pork Loin with Quinoa: Flavor the pork loin (5 ounces raw weight) with 2 to 3 shakes of dried rosemary and ½ teaspoon minced garlic. Grill or broil pork loin for about 20 minutes, or until brown inside. Cook quinoa (¼ cup dry) in vegetable or chicken broth and a dash of cumin. Toss with ½ cup mushrooms and 1 tablespoon chopped green onions sautéed in 1 tablespoon whipped butter. **2 cups steamed broccoli**	491	26.8 g	41.3 g	15.2 g
TOTAL	**1,518**	**164.8 g** (43%)	**109.2 g** (29%)	**37.7 g** (22%)

{ I DID IT! } ►

Name: Tiffany Moore

Age: 26

Town: Madison Heights, Virginia

Weight Lost: 12 pounds

Other Accomplishments: Shrank her waist by 6 inches and went from a size 8 to a size 3

before   after

"I was once slim enough to work as a model, but a few years of eating too much junk and fast food and exercising too little began to creep up on me. When I got engaged and my fiancé and I set our wedding date for February 15, 2003, I decided to lose about 10 pounds in order to fit into my dream gown.

"It took me about 3 months to lose around 12 pounds. Not only did I fit into that wedding gown, I've kept the weight off since. I've lost more weight since my wedding, now weighing in at only 112! I've lost about 6 inches from my waist, and I went from a size 8 to a size 3. I have toned up a lot. I used to wear medium-size shirts, and now I can wear a small and even possibly get away with an extra-small.

"I exercise with the stability ball and have seen amazing results, particularly for my abs. I always work out in the morning before I get ready for work. That way, my workout is done for the day. Plus it gives me a lot of energy for the rest of the day. I sometimes work out again in the evenings if I've consumed more calories than I burned off that day.

"In addition to exercise, I also eat a very healthy diet. I consume between 1,200 and 1,400 calories a day (sometimes more), drink at least 64 ounces of water a day, and eat my five servings of fruits and veggies a day. Since I've been at my current weight, I feel great about myself! I have so much more energy and motivation! I owe it all to Denise!"

Tiffany's Advice: Use photos to motivate yourself. Tiffany has placed a photo of herself at her lowest weight near her alarm clock, to help her get out of bed in the morning for her workout. "I also have a picture of Denise on my dresser," she says. "I want to be that fit when I'm in my forties!"

◄ . . . .

SHOPPING LISTS

I look at preparation time as a gift I give to myself—time to press the "reset" button and recharge for the coming week. I hope these shopping lists will help you make the most of your preparation time. Lists help me stick to my plan and avoid making last-minute choices that could sabotage my goals. Just photocopy these lists and take them with you on your weekly grocery shopping trips.

WEEK 1 SHOPPING LIST

Produce
Apples, 2
Asparagus, 1 small bunch
Berries, frozen, 2 large bags (buy 2 different
    kinds and mix)
Broccoli, 1 head
Celery, 1 bag
Cucumber, 1 small
Garlic, 1 bulb (enough for 3 weeks)
Gingerroot, 1 (keep in the freezer)
Grapefruit, 1
Green beans, ¼ pound
Italian vegetables, frozen, 1 bag
Kiwifruit, 1
Melon, 1
Mushrooms, fresh (¼ pound) or canned
    (8 ounces)
Onion, red, 1 small
Onion, white or yellow, 1
Onions, green, 1 small bunch
Oranges, 2
Oriental vegetables, frozen, 1 bag
Pears, 2
Pepper, red bell, 1

Peppers, roasted red, 1 small jar
Potato, Idaho, 1
Potatoes, sweet, 2
Radishes, 1 bag
Salad greens, 1 bag
Spinach, baby, 1 bag
Tangerines, 3
Tomatoes, fresh, 2
Tomatoes, sun-dried, 1 container
Vegetable juice, 1 bottle
Water chestnuts, 1 small can

Dairy
Butter, whipped, 1 container
Cottage cheese, low-fat, 12 ounces
Eggs, 1 dozen
Milk, fat-free, 1 quart
Parmesan cheese (enough for 3 weeks)
Romano cheese, 8 ounces
String cheese, 1 package
Swiss cheese, ¼ pound
Yogurt, light, any flavor, 2 single-serving
    (8-ounce) containers

Meat, Poultry, and Seafood

Canadian bacon, 1 package (keep in freezer, buy sliced)

Chicken breast, skinless, boneless, 1½ pounds

Flank steak, 1 pound

Ham, ⅓ pound shaved

Salmon, 1 (8-ounce) piece

Salmon, smoked, 1 package

Tuna, 1 (3-ounce) can

Turkey bacon, 1 package

Turkey breast, ground, ½ pound

Grains

Barley, 1 box

Bow-tie pasta, whole wheat, 1 package

Cereal, high-fiber, 1 box (enough for 3 weeks)

English muffins, 1 package

Oatmeal, instant or regular, 1 box

Pita, whole wheat (2 ounces each), 1 package

Popcorn kernels, I jar

Quinoa, 1 small bag

Rice, brown, 1 box (enough for 3 weeks)

Rolls, whole grain (2¼ inches), 2

Tortillas, corn or whole wheat (6-inch diameter), 1 package (freeze)

Other (will last for 3 weeks)

Almonds, 1 bag (keep in airtight container)

Black pepper, 1 container

Capers, 1 small jar

Cayenne pepper, 1 container

Cinnamon, 1 container

Garlic powder, 1 container

Hot-pepper sauce, 1 jar

Hummus, 1 small container

Italian seasoning, 1 container

Mayonnaise, low-fat, 1 small jar

Mustard, country, spicy, Dijon, raspberry, horseradish, or regular, 1 jar

Old Bay seasoning, 1 container

Olive oil, 1 bottle

Onion soup mix, 1 box

Peanut butter, chunky, 1 small jar

Raspberry vinaigrette, 1 bottle

Red wine vinaigrette, 1 bottle

Salad dressing, light, any flavor, 1 bottle

Salsa, 1 large jar (enough for 3 weeks)

Sea salt, 1 container

Soybeans, roasted, 1 container

Soy sauce, low-sodium, 1 bottle

Spaghetti sauce, 1 jar

Syrup, light, 1 bottle

Tofu, silken, 1 (8-ounce) package

Tomato soup, 1 (10¾-ounce) can

Vegetable soup, 1 (10¾-ounce) can

Vegetable spray, 1 can

Worcestershire sauce, 1 bottle

WEEK 2 SHOPPING LIST

Produce
Apples, 2
Basil, 1 bunch
Broccoli, 1 head
Cantaloupe, 1
Chickpeas, 1 (8-ounce) can
Cucumber, 1
Grapefruit, 1
Green beans, ¼ pound
Kidney beans, 1 (14½-ounce) can
Kiwifruit, 2
Lemon, 1
Mango, 1
Mushrooms, 2 small cans
Mushrooms, fresh, ¼ pound
Onion, white or yellow, 1
Oranges, 2
Parsley, 1 small bunch
Pepper, red bell, 1
Potatoes, sweet, 2
Salad greens, 1 bag
Shallot, 1
Spinach, baby, 1 bag
Sugar snap peas, ½ pound
Tangerine, 1
Tomatoes, flavored and diced, 1 (26-ounce) can
Tomatoes, fresh, 2
Tomatoes, grape, 1 container
Vegetable juice, 1 bottle
Zucchinis, 2

Dairy
Cheddar cheese, light, shredded, 1 bag
Cottage cheese, low-fat, 12 ounces
Eggs, 6
Milk, fat-free, 1 quart
Yogurt, light, any flavor, 2 single-serving
    (8-ounce) containers

Meat, Poultry, and Seafood
Chicken breast tenderloins, 1 package
Ham, baked, ¼ pound sliced or shaved
Salmon, smoked, 1 small package
Shrimp, baby, frozen, 1 bag
Sirloin, extra-lean, 1 pound
Tuna, 1 (8-ounce) piece
Turkey breast, peppered, ¼ pound (from deli)

Grains
Bread, whole grain, 1 loaf (freeze)
Cereal, toasted oats, 1 box
Rolls, whole grain (2¼ inches), 2
Stuffed shells, light, frozen, 1 package
Stuffing mix, 1 box
Tortilla chips, baked, 1 small bag

Other
Allspice or nutmeg, 1 container
Balsamic vinegar, 1 bottle
Chili powder, 1 container
Fruit spread, 1 jar
Lentil soup, 1 (10½-ounce) can
Olives, green, 1 small jar
Peanuts, 1 ounce
Relish, 1 small jar
Teriyaki sauce, 1 bottle

WEEK 3 SHOPPING LIST

Produce

Apples, 3
Asparagus, 1 pound
Black beans, 1 can
Broccoli, 1 head
Chunky vegetables, frozen, 1 bag
Cucumbers, 2
Grapefruit, 2
Green beans, ¼ pound
Jalapeño, 1 (optional)
Kiwifruit, 1
Lemon, 1
Mushrooms, 1 can
Onion, red, 1
Onions, green, 1 small bunch
Onions, white or yellow, 3
Oranges, 2
Parsley, 1 small bunch
Pears, 2
Peppers, red or green bell, 2 large
Portobello mushrooms, 2
Potato, Idaho, 1
Rosemary, fresh (1 small bunch) or dried
    (1 bottle)
Salad greens, 1 bag
Shallot, 1
Sugar snap peas, ¼ pound
Tangerines, 2
Tomato, fresh, 1
Tomatoes, flavored and diced, 1 can
Tomatoes, grape, 2 containers
Zucchini, 1

Dairy

Cottage cheese, low-fat, 12 ounces
Eggs, 6
Feta cheese, crumbled, 1 package
Milk, fat-free, 1 quart
Provolone, ¼ pound
Ricotta cheese, light, 1 small container
Yogurt, light, any flavor, 4 single-serving
    (8-ounce) containers

Meat, Poultry, and Seafood

Canadian bacon, 1 package
Chicken breast, skinless, boneless, 1 pound
Frozen light entrée with chicken or beef
Pork loin, 16 ounces raw weight
Roughy, 1 (8-ounce) piece
Salmon, 1 (3-ounce) can
Tofu, silken, 8 ounces
Tuna, 1 (6-ounce) piece
Turkey breast, ground, ½ pound
Turkey breast, smoked, ¼ pound (from deli)

Grains

Bulgur, 1 small box
Penne pasta, whole wheat, 1 package
Roll, whole grain (2¼ inches), 1
Tortellini, spinach, 1 package
Waffles, whole grain, 1 box

Other

Bean dip, 1 (8-ounce) jar
Cumin, 1 container
Dillweed, 1 container
Ginger teriyaki sauce, 1 bottle
Horseradish, 1 jar
Pesto, refrigerated, 1 small container
Sunflower seeds, 1 small bag
Vegetable soup, 1 (10¾-ounce) can
Vegetable soup mix, 1 package

INDEX

Boldface page references indicate illustrations and photographs.

Underscored references indicate boxed text.

Posture
    cobra posture for improving, 164, **164**
    during exercises, 85
    importance of strong core muscles for, 17
    stability ball influence on, 17
    stretching for improvement in, 112
    upper-body sculpting and, 83–84
Potato recipe, 222
Poultry, shopping list for
    week 1, 294
    week 2, 295
    week 3, 296
Power, from strong core muscles, 17
Pregnancy, effect on abdominal muscles, 31–32
Priorities, setting, 11–12
Produce, shopping list for
    week 1, 293
    week 2, 295
    week 3, 296
Protein, 195, 280
Pump, 20, 21–22
Pushup, 88–89, **88–89**

Q

Quadriceps, 56, 184
Quad sets, 76–77, **76–77**
Quality, over quantity, 4
Quinoa, 290

R

Range of motion, 6, 18
Recipes
    breakfast
        Berry Smoothie, 282
        Blueberry Smoothie, 214
        Breakfast BT Sandwich, 256
        Breakfast Burrito, 206
        Breakfast Parfait, 262
        Crunchy Cinnamon Oatmeal, 290
        Ham and Cheddar Breakfast Sandwich, 244
        Mexican Egg Sandwich, 266
        Smoked Salmon and Egg Pita, 248
        Spiced Oatmeal, 252
        Strawberry Smoothie, 236
        Sweet and Crunchy Oatmeal, 210
    dinner
        Asparagus Spears, 218
        Baked Sweet Potato, 240
        Bow-Tie Pasta and Asparagus, 226
        Chicken and Vegetable Stir-Fry, 206

Chicken Parmesan, 226
Chicken Quesadillas, 286
Chili, 236
Flank Steak, 222
Foil-Baked Herbed Chicken Breast, 266
Garlic Potatoes, 222
Ginger Teriyaki Tuna with Bulgur, 274
Italian Omelet, 214
Italian Vegetable Frittata, 256
Mango Spinach Salad, 256
Penne with Ricotta and Spinach, 282
Pork Loin with Barley, 270
Pork Loin with Quinoa, 290
Roasted Vegetables, 266
Salmon with Salsa and Capers, 210
Shrimp Stir-Fry, 248
Spicy Turkey Burger, 218
Spinach Cheese Tortellini with Feta,
    Tomatoes, Salmon, and Pesto, 262
Spinach Salad, 278
Stuffed Chicken Breast, 252
Stuffed Peppers, 278
Tomato-Topped Roughy, 282
Tuna and Vegetable Teriyaki Kebabs, 240
Turkey and Mixed Greens Salad, 232
lunch
    Flank Steak Fajita, 232
    Fresh Veggie Salad, 252
    Ham and Cheese Pita, 222
    Lentil and Tomato Soup, 256
    Marinated Vegetable Salad, 282
    Mushroom Omelet, 226
    Onion and Mushroom Omelet, 286
    Portobello Mushrooms, 278
    Salmon Pita, 236
    Salmon Salad, 270
    Shrimp and Spinach Salad, 244
    Spinach Salad, 218
    Stir-Fry Wrap, 214
    Stuffed Chicken Salad, 262
    Stuffed Shells, 244
    Tortellini Salad, 266
    Tuna Pita, 206
    Turkey Wrap, 290
Reciprocal reach, 54, **54**
Rectus abdominis muscle, 16, 32
Resistance bands. *See also specific exercises*
    with attachments, 20
    benefits for joints, 18
    buying variety of, 20
    cleaning, 22
    combining with stability ball, 6, 16

Week 3 (*cont.*)
    day 20, 280–82
    day 21, 284–86
    day 22, 288–90
    shopping lists, 296
Weekly program, designing, 188–90
Weigh-in, 201, 231, 254, 261, 289
Wheel posture, 154, 167, **167**
Workout
    adding to, 212
    amount of time needed, 7–8
    clothing, 23
    convenience, 8–9, 18
    crucial elements
        cardio plan, customized, 9
        Daily Dozen toning routine, 9
        eating plan, 9–10
        rejuvenating rest, 10
    Daily Dozen
        week 1, **205, 209, 213, 217, 221, 225**
        week 2, **235, 239, 243, 247, 251, 255**
        week 3, **265, 269, 273, 277, 281, 285**
    goals of, 171
    marking on calendar, 13
    mini, 13, 18
    routine design
        circuit workout, <u>188</u>
        core muscles, 185–86, <u>186</u>, <u>187</u>

        efficiency, 180
        lower-body, 184–85, <u>184</u>, <u>185</u>
        total-body, 187–88
        upper-body, 182–83, <u>182</u>, <u>183</u>
        weekly program, 188–90
    space design, 22–23
    starting day with, 8, <u>26</u>
    variety in, 170–71, 173, 238

Y

Yoga
    breathing, 154
    mat, 23
    postures
        balancing stick, 153, 162, **162**
        bridge, 165, **165**
        cobra, 154, 164, **164**
        forward bend, 27, 166, **166**
        knee sway, 154, 169, **169**
        mermaid, 154, 163, **163**
        pose of the dancer, 153, 155, **155**
        threading the needle, 168, **168**
        triangle, 153, 160–61, **160–61**
        warrior 1, 153, 156–57, **156–57**
        warrior 2, 153, 158–59, **158–59**
        wheel, 154, 167, **167**
    target areas, 153–54